The Preacher's Ideals
and Inspirations

Lectures on the George Shepard Foundation
Bangor Convocation, 1916

The Preacher's Ideals and Inspirations

By

WILLIAM J. HUTCHINS

*Professor of Homiletics in the Oberlin Graduate
School of Theology*

NEW YORK   CHICAGO   TORONTO
Fleming H. Revell Company
LONDON   AND   EDINBURGH

251R
H97

108772

To
MY FATHER

Foreword

THE addresses which make up this book were prepared not for the extraordinary preacher, but for the average man who in a small parish in the face of grave difficulties tries to continue true to the dreams of his youth, to the teachings of his seminary days, and to the demands of the living present.

The lecture on Abraham Lincoln was given to an evening audience in which laymen predominated.

The colloquial style of spoken address has been retained in the hope that it may bring to the reader a little of the atmosphere of frank comradeship which pervaded all the gatherings of the Convocation.

I cannot fittingly express my gratitude to the President and Faculty of Bangor Seminary, and to the friends made at the Convocation, whose friendship is a permanent asset of my life.

W. J. H.

Oberlin, Ohio.

Contents

I

The Preacher and His Times

I

THE PREACHER AND HIS TIMES

AS a man looks through a preacher's eyes at the life of our times, there seems at first much to dishearten him. We turn back with envy to the great days of the Puritans, when men actually went to church. Old Judge Sewall writes in his diary, "Extraordinary cold storm of wind and rain; blows much more as coming home, and holds on," or again, "Bread was frozen at the Lord's table, yet was very comfortable at meeting." If we could only have been preachers then! We read long articles about the workingman's indifference or hostility to the Church. Edward Lewis, himself a minister and formerly a pastor, writes of the Church as a diminishing and decaying institution from which power and authority in the world are swiftly passing. We are continually reminded that the Church is ecclesiastical bric-à-brac. The query is raised, Has the Church collapsed? Are we to have a constituency for Christianity?

In a preachers' magazine I read of the

13

Rout of the Theological Seminaries, and the imagination conjured up the spectacle of faculties, theologues and buildings, all swiftly decomposing into a heterogeneous mass to form some lateral moraine along the margin of the glacial stream of history. At last a man who has honestly identified his life with the life of the Church and the ministry reminds himself of the old soldier beggar, who bore upon his breast this legend: " Have pity on me, been in five battles, wounded twice, children four, total eleven." But just as we have voted, unanimously, that the Church and especially the ministers and preeminently the seminaries have descended to Avernus, there appear above the horizon certain facts, which force us to move a reconsideration of our question. I might remind you of certain facts of history; for example in 1803, so great and good a man as the first President Dwight of Yale declared, " We have a country governed by blockheads and knaves. Who can paint anything more dreadful this side of hell?" It was at this very time that the lower courses of the fair structure of our Republic were being laid. Writing in 1851, Amiel said, " The age of great men is going, the epoch of the ant-hill is beginning. The statistician will register a growing progress, and the

moralist a gradual decline." Yet this epoch
of the ant-hill was the epoch of Webster and
of Lincoln, of the men who were to create
America's golden age. From the beginning of recorded history there have been
great and good men who have sat raven-like
upon the pallid bust of the mighty past, and
muttered their "Nevermore." Macaulay,
you remember, said, "All my days I have
seen nothing but progress and heard of nothing but decay."

But I prefer to speak to you of certain
facts of the present. And the first fact, a
most hopeful fact, is the current discontent in
the industrial and in the religious world,
technically so called. In the industrial world
the discontent reveals itself indeed in strikes,
lockouts, murders. In the "religious" world
the discontent is less conspicuous ; it is none
the less real. While educated Japan throws
away her idols for the worship of the emperor
or the worship of nothing; while China
throws her gods into the river ; while India
is being stirred to scepticism of the ancient
systems ; with us religious discontent reveals
itself in the ceaseless search for some new
thing, or in the total disregard of all organized religion.

Now the encouraging feature of the current discontent is this: Almost invariably it

is discontent with the unchristlike aspects of
our life and thought. I know that there are
Pharisees intent upon maintaining the present
status who will deny this. I know too that
there are men intent upon winning pleasure,
leisure, treasure, who would seem to disprove
the assertion, but speaking broadly we are
convinced the statement is true. Men refuse
to rest content, as they look upon New York
" reeling crazy drunk with money," and look
upon New Yorkers staggering with starva-
tion. They rise in wrath against a Christian
civilization which in a single year kills nearly
three thousand of those who in the darkness
of the earth bring to the earth's surface
Emerson's "portable climate," a civilization
which in a recent year killed or injured nearly
200,000 people on its steam and electric rail-
ways, a civilization of bread lines and limou-
sines. They scorn a commerce which as an
author says, "holds in one hand the slum
and in the other the mission field ; " a commerce which might still lead a candid observer
to approve the course of the Indian chief of
Cuba, who, I read, ordered his people to worship a lump of gold to conciliate the white
man's God. Men will not believe that a
Church rent by discord can fitly represent the
body of Christ. The prevalent discontent is
discontent with those aspects of our thought

and life which are out of harmony with the
life and teachings of Jesus Christ.   And who
is He?   He is the sole Lord and Leader of
the Christian preacher.

Another most encouraging feature of the
life of our times is the failure of panaceas.
Industrial and political panaceas have been
as numerous as the demons who once in-
habited the swine of Gadara, and who, you
recall, drove their possessors into the sea.
In those regions in which the panaceas have
been tried most faithfully, they have been
found at best to alleviate, never to eradicate
the real evils of the world's life.   I remind
you of Australia, where until the Great War
set men upon nobler issues, money love and
pleasure love threatened to strangle the life
out of men.   "In America," says Jefferson,
"we have suffered a heart-breaking disillu-
sionment.   We expected great things of
liberty and education, and have found them
broken reeds.   Neither our wealth nor our
science has given us peace or joy.   The four
wizards, liberty and education and wealth
and science, have performed their mightiest
miracles under our flag, but they cannot do
the one thing essential, they cannot keep the
conscience quick or the soul alive to God."
We can now send the recognizable human
voice over 4,600 miles of land and sea, but

what if that voice shall but echo the death cries of Poland or Armenia?

Nor has the "religious" world been without her panaceas. Ever and again some Aaron erects his altar and upon it places his particular pet calf, and cries to our wandering Israel, "This is thy god which shall lead thee up out of Egypt!" But notwithstanding seeming temporary success, every one of these panaceas fails, because it fails to deal radically with the radical problem of all religion. And that is what? Sin. I have understood that Dr. Shedd's theology is somewhat out of date. He says at least one true word: "A profound consciousness of sin in the heart, and a correspondingly profound theory of sin in the head are fundamental to any soundness of view in the general domain of theology." And a religious panacea which knows no consciousness of sin in the hearts of men, and offers for the heads of men no theory of sin, but sin's denial, has no healing for the hurt of the daughter of my people.

Now what is the meaning of this universal discontent, so deep seated, so pathetic? What is the meaning of this failure of panaceas? You have seen a little lost child brought into a police station. The big friendly officers do their best to still his sob-

bings; they cannot do it.   Kindly neighbour
women come, try to still his sobbings, but
they cannot do it.   At last a woman rushes
in, clasps the child to her arms, and the baby
is at rest.   Perhaps he cannot tell why.   The
reason is that he has found his mother.
Blind, unconsoled, humanity seeks for a
Saviour, and unless this world of ours is a
mad-house, humanity shall find the Saviour
and in His arms be at rest; but not yet has
any man discovered a name under heaven
given among men, by which humanity can
be saved, other than the name of Him who
is the sole Lord and Leader of the Christian
preacher.

Further, as we study the life of our times,
we are impressed by a wonderful new aspiration, the aspiration after brotherhood.   That
seems to me a significant story, which Mott
tells.   A Scotch soldier was brought into the
hospital.   He was holding fiercely in his hand
a German helmet and would not let it go.
" Did you kill him ?" said the nurse.   " No,
he was my friend; " and then the boy told
how, when he was wounded so that he could
not help himself, he chanced to see a German soldier, wounded so that he could not
help himself.   Each crawled slowly towards
the other, each staunched the other's wounds,

each saved the other's life; and when they were carried to their separate hospitals, the Scotch boy gave the German his cap and the German gave the Scotch lad his helmet, for that day on that field of death they knew that they were brothers. The man who wrote the " Chant of Hate " would to-day, I suspect, willingly suppress it. You read the word of a military officer after the first Christmas of the war: " Another such day, and our troops will quit and go home." If you give them but the chance to know each other, you cannot make men, manly men, persistently hate each other.

In labour circles, men are achieving a very real if a very partial brotherhood. Surely the class-conscious struggle is a passing phase. Until with the beginning of " the great mad war," professors lost all sense of humour, and began sending back home their degrees and decorations, we had grown familiar with the fine brotherhood of men of letters. All truth, wherever learned, used to be, and will once more become, " the property of men of thought throughout the world." Pan-Americanism is a prophecy; internationalism is a hope. There are millions of men who are daring to cry, " Above all nations, humanity." Ecclesiastical federation is in the air. The World

Conference of Faith and Order may summon
us to something closer than federation.   Our
Canadian brothers, our missionaries in China,
India and Japan, are shaming our sects at
home into some semblance of unity.

As you go up and down the country, are
you not continually delighted and humbled
as you think upon the number of " good people," as we call them, men whom you meet
unexpectedly, to find that they are brotherly
men, caring for the things you care for, loving the things you love ?   As you meet some
crisis of your life you are amazed at the number of people who quietly, unostentatiously
but aggressively, do the loving brotherly
thing.

I think of that story of the Civil War.   The
Confederates were storming some Union for-
tifications.   In the ascent of the hill, they
reached a gully, from which they could not
move.   The wounded were dying of thirst.
A lad of eighteen gathered all the empty
canteens he could carry and slipped like
a snake to the foot of the hill and filled
the canteens at the brook.   He must hurry
back in full sight of the men on the fortifica-
tions.   The Union soldiers saw him, but they
saw also his purpose, and there burst from
the ramparts a volley, not of rifle shots, but
of cheers for the man who would die for his

brothers. Never has there been a time when brotherhood was so dear to men, and men there are whom we count enemies of the brotherly life, who in their hearts applaud, approve, and long to be like the man who pays the price of brotherhood.

Already the aspiration after brotherhood has become a majestic movement. Put your ear to the ground and you hear its watchwords. In the world of business, you hear two strange old-fashioned words, Honesty, Service, words actually made a slogan by the advertising men of America, except, one would judge, by the advertisers of cigarettes and of whiskey. In the world of international politics, above the noise of battle you hear clear and distinct the watchword, Peace. In the world of ecclesiastics you hear louder than the echoes of the Kikuyu controversy, the watchword, Unity. In the world of social life, you hear just one watchword, Social Salvation, the Redemption of Society. One man seeks to foster rural reconstruction, another the social hygiene of the city, another calls us to a crusade of brotherhood on behalf of the negro. A while ago a modest man, graduate of Western Reserve University, began to think about the immigrants streaming into the city of his alma mater. He took a camera and caught

upon his films the evidences of the chicanery
and brutality of cabmen towards the immigrants coming into the city, and that obscure
man soon found the courts of law, the public
institutions, the municipal offices of Cleveland, not obstacles to, but vehicles of social
redemption.

Consider the times in which we live, times
which furnish an atmosphere for the carrying
of such watchwords as these.   Suppose that
in the time of Frederick the Great a man
had uttered such words; he would have
spoken in a vacuum, there would have been
no atmosphere to carry them.   Yet each one
of these watchwords, Honesty, Service, Peace,
Unity, Social Salvation, is one word of the
evangel of Jesus Christ, the sole Lord and
Leader of the Christian preacher.

Along with this new aspiration we observe
as an encouraging fact of our times a new
emphasis, the emphasis upon personality.
We are coming to discount creeds, institutions, constitutions as such.   We are coming
to recognize the imperious need of the man,
the man who can "lift 'em, lift 'em, lift 'em,
through the charge that wins the day."   In
America we have been obsessed by the idea
of salvation by legislation ; but the obsession
passes.   The thirteenth, fourteenth and fif-

teenth amendments to the Constitution leave the Negro a slave except in name. Up from slavery he must be led by men, by Armstrong and Booker Washington and their comrades. Before 1902 we had laws enough to make all business honest, but a man was needed to organize the ethical revolution, in the midst of which we are still fighting. Again and again that word of wide application comes back to a man, " What the Law could not do." We are forced to appreciate anew the word of Isaiah: "A man," not a creed, "a man," not an institution, "a man," not a constitution, "a man shall be as a hiding place from the wind and a covert from the tempest, as streams of water in a dry place, as the shade of a great rock in a weary land." Now what is the meaning of this new emphasis upon personality? Any complete reliance on any human being brings into fatal publicity the pathetic weakness of the man. I suppose that Asquith, Balfour, and Lloyd George are the strongest men in England. They seem like swimmers struggling against the currents of Hell Gate. I suppose that the Kaiser is the strongest man on the continent. How puny is the power of a man who even if victorious must bleed his country white. As the world grows thoughtful, is not the world getting ready to trust the personality of *the* Man who once walked in Galilee, whose touch hath still its ancient power, "man's best Man, love's best Love, the perfect life in perfect labour writ, all men's Comrade, Servant, King or Priest," even Jesus Christ, the sole Lord and Leader of the Christian preacher?

> " In his life, the Law appears
> Drawn out in living characters."

Again we are impressed by certain new appreciations. There is in our times a new appreciation of religion. One is perfectly safe in talking of religion with any man one meets upon the street. You recall that word of a friend to Justice Holmes of the Supreme Court: "There is only one interesting thing in the world, and that is religion." Men are finding that out. When we are all through talking about baseball and football and preparedness and the war itself, the one permanently, fundamentally interesting thing in the world is religion. The crowds will throng a park, mechanics will pack a shop meeting, taking time from their lunch-hour to hear a man of God as he gives his word from God. Revivalists are heard with all the old time relish even when they speak in coarse, crude language of God and sin, and death and life eternal. If Billy Sunday were speaking upon any other theme in the world, could he begin to draw the crowds which flock to hear him?

Slowly, too, men are coming to appreciate not alone the supreme interest of religion, but its supreme importance. Amos prophesies a great famine in the land, not a famine of bread, nor a thirst for water but of hearing the words of Jehovah. Well, the famine has come to many men. To any well fed and healthy soul, there are essential reason and hope and love and the choice of the highest. No word from God! The reason asks the question Why? Why am I here? What's the meaning of life? What's the meaning of growth? What's the meaning of the persistent upward look of men? What's the secret of the great personalities who have led and liberated the generations? No word from God! The reason starves.

As the reason considers the great personalities of the world, love reaches out to embrace them. Love unless perverted seeks the loveliest. But these loveliest take us by the hand and lead us up to—God? But now there is no word from God, and love is stunned and starved.

To a healthy soul, there are essential great hopes. When we are at our best we dare to hope that no paradise stands barred to entry.

We dare even to hope for personal immortality for ourselves and those we call our friends.

Van Dyke, standing by the grave of his friend Stedman, says :

> " You followed through the quest of life,
>   The light that shines above
> The tumult and the toil of men,
>   And shows us what to love.
>
> " Right loyal to the best you knew,
>   Reality or dream,
> You ran the race, you fought the fight,
>   A follower of the Gleam.
>
> " We lay upon your folded hands
>   The wreath of asphodel ;
> We speak above your peaceful face
>   The tender word *Farewell !*
>
> " For well you fare, in God's good care,
>   Somewhere within the blue,
> And know, to-day, your dearest dreams
>   Are true,—and true,—and true ! "

But now there is no word from God. So far as we know, our dearest dreams are false and false and false.

When we are at our best we dare to hope for the ideal civilization. Indeed we think we see it coming. Out of the chaotic kaleidoscopic elements of the present we believe that we can see arising a cosmos, a fair and ordered and beautiful thing. But now there is no word from God. The hopes that make us men begin to wither in our hearts.

And as we hope, we choose. There have been those who supposed that if there were no word from God men could be persuaded still to choose the good and eschew the evil. It is very far from certain. We have often marked the word of the Japanese Minister of Home Affairs to the representatives of the three great religions of Japan, Buddhism, Shintoism and Christianity: "Teach well your religions." Why? Scandals, suicides, social deterioration have made it clear to the elder statesmen of Japan that an ethics unsupported by religion is a house built on the sand.

"Drink, for you know not whence you came nor why.
Drink, for you know not why you go, nor where."

Jane Addams has publicly declared that were she to enter again upon her gracious work, she would use more largely, more positively, the redemptive forces of religion.

With this new appreciation of religion, its interest and importance, there is a new and profound appreciation of Jesus, not necessarily of the Christ of our orthodox faith, but a new appreciation of Jesus, His teachings, His character, His regal authority in the realm of spirit.

We have not forgotten the blackguard speech of the representative of the anti-

Christian Socialist League of England:
"Many of the parsons or modern medicine
men, flunkies of the supernatural, have been
seriously troubled by the people falling away
from Christism. Politics have been attract-
ing the working people more and more, religion less and less. For this reason the
reverend hypocrites have suddenly discovered
that Jesus was a socialist. Christ's teaching
is antagonistic to all sound morality and
sound progress. Human freedom and hap-
piness can only be obtained by repudiating
Christism of all kinds and all its works."
But this utterance is so exceptional as to be
almost unique. It has been well said, "His
name is great among the Gentiles." Labour
agitators, communists, socialists all do Him
reverence. The Jew scarcely finds words to
express his devotion to the man Jesus.
Rabbi Kohler, in opening a Jewish Congress
in 1893, exclaimed, "Jesus the keeper of the
poor, the friend of the sinner, the brother of
the sufferer, the comfort of the sorrow laden,
the healer of the sick, the uplifter of the
fallen, the lover of men, the redeemer of
women, we [we Jews] claim him as our
own." You have noticed the sinister suggestion that during the war a moratorium on
Christianity be proclaimed. You read the
question presented in Parliament: "As there

is nothing doing in Christianity at present, isn't it important that clergymen should enlist?" But do not words like these simply throw into clearer relief the conviction of men that as the present collapse of civilization is the fruit of unchristlike international relations, so the proper organization of political and social life involves the enthronement of the principles and purposes of Jesus?

What does the new appreciation of religion, the new appreciation of Jesus mean? Surely this, a growing acceptance of Jesus, until He shall be crowned King of kings and Lord of lords. But Jesus Christ, I repeat, is the sole Lord and Leader of the Christian preacher.

The times clamour for those " durable satisfactions" which our Lord and Leader alone can bring to men.

As the preacher estimates his times, he is compelled to ask how the times estimate him. Am I as preacher equipped to mediate to the times the durable satisfactions for which they cry?

It is argued that the magazine, the newspaper, the moving picture show, the book, have supplanted the preacher in the instruction of the people. We may take comfort from the remark reported of the late H. R.

Haweis, to the effect that "in the persistence
of preaching is a conspicuous example of the
survival of the fittest.   If preaching could
have been killed, it would have been killed
long ago by the thousands of imbecile
sermons that have been poured from count-
less pulpits throughout the ages of the
Church."   A keen observer has said that in
no country whatever is a genius for public
speaking a more useful and commanding
endowment than in America.   Men do not
like to listen to dullards, but men still delight
to listen to the man who utters truth through
personality.   A Congregational minister in
the middle west has as good a moving picture
apparatus as is to be found in the state.   He
tells me that in the long run the preacher can
beat the pictures.   As contrasted with the
speaking man how ineffective is the written
page.   Professor Palmer said to his wife,
Alice Freeman Palmer : "When you are
gone, people will ask who you were, and
nobody will be able to say."   "Why should
they say?   I am trying to make girls wiser
and happier.   Books don't help much towards
that.   They are entertaining enough, but
really dead things.   Why should I make
more of them?   It is people that count.
You want to put yourself into people ; they
touch other people, these others still, and so

you go on working forever." "This speaking one—there is need of him yet."

It is argued that the prejudice against the Church precludes the wide hearing of the preacher's message. There is prejudice against the Church, but one notes with interest that Montana chambers of commerce still regard the presence of churches as one of the best advertisements of boom towns. We are to become increasingly familiar with such rebukes as that which a socialist leader addressed to an irate comrade who was inveighing against the Church: "Cut out those attacks on the Church. They're doing the best they know how, and I believe they are trying to give us a square deal." One of the most biting of the recent critics of the Church says, "Let not the reader think of me as a spiteful critic of the churches. Far from it; I believe that they are the hope of the world, and carry its future." The prejudice against the Church is almost invariably directed against the Church as it is, not as it ought to be, can be, as by God's help it shall be. The statistics of the churches for the year 1915 tend to confirm the belief that as people begin to think, they begin to turn not from the churches but towards them. There is a growing recognition of the fact which another has stated: "Break up the Christian As-

sembly for a generation and Christ's grip
upon the nations is broken."

But it is insisted that there is not the old
time respect for "the cloth." No, thank God,
there is not. In other days the "cloth"
might cover a menagerie of clean and un-
clean beasts. To-day the cloth is respected
if and only if it happens to cover a man. But
then, how greatly is it respected. Easily the
first citizen of Columbus, Ohio, is a minister.
Was not Edward Everett Hale the first
citizen of Boston? It is more than possible
that the first citizen of your own town is a
minister. Certainly the first citizen of many
a town and hamlet in this broad country is a
minister of Christ. If any man dreams that
there is not a present day respect for the man-
covering cloth, he may do well to consider the
efforts of the liquor dealers to make the cloth
cover one of their spokesmen. President
Wilson did not think he was wasting his time
when he made the journey from Washington
to Columbus simply for the sake of expressing
his interest in the rural church. Nor did he
think that he or his cause lost influence when
he confessed that he was the son of a country
preacher.

But surely the preacher has lost much of
his power in the community because the
higher criticism has disintegrated the faith

of men? It is to be confessed that the two decades before 1910 were hard days for the younger men in the ministry. Historical criticism has done and is doing a work which simply cannot be undone. Much rubbish has been removed. Strong and massive rise the preachable truths of our religion; Jesus Christ, the unveiling of God the Father, saviour from sin, founder and pioneer of the civilization of brotherly men, prince of the eternal life. What would one have?

"But do you not think that the preacher's field has been invaded and largely occupied by various modern organizations, the Associations of young men and young women, the social settlement, the neighbourhood house and the rest?" We need scarcely be reminded that every one of these enterprises is the child of the Church. Not one of them could live for five years without the help of the Church. A friend of mine well says: "It is easy to drink of a stream, and to forget the source." But as all of these organizations are the constant beneficiaries of the Church, practically all of them are now the willing allies or rather auxiliaries of the Church. The representatives of these organizations invariably have to explain themselves or plead for their right to exist in a community, the priest-prophet never. His

function is as old as the family, and will pass
when there is no man left to hear his message.

The New York *Evening Post* is not the
organ of the Intermediate Endeavour Society,
nor is it the advertising agent of any theological seminary. You may have read this
significant editorial : " Christianity has been
preëminently the preached religion. In-
spired preaching has in it the greatest power
known to man, that of a kindled personality.
It is the most potent fascination which anything external in the Church can wield, more
vivid than music, more direct than even
grand architecture, and fit adornment of
the temple. We ourselves believe that the
dearth of great preachers is only temporary.
The high themes are there, the human heart
remains the same, the opportunity and the
aspiration appeal to lofty natures as of old.
We shall once more hear the sincere and
moving voices, which from the beginning till
now have best carried Christian truth to the
hearts and minds of men."

But to pass from questions to assertions that
can scarcely be questioned. The preacher is
set to instruct and inspire the one organization which is commissioned and equipped to
preserve, to interpret and to proclaim to our
times the book which has rightly been called
the Word of God. We gladly remember

that a few of our colleges and both of our Christian Associations are giving some instruction in the Bible. At the best they reach only an infinitesimal part of the population. The Bible is practically banished from our public schools. Where its use is permitted, it is usually read, not studied. We shall have occasion later to consider the certain disaster which would accompany the loss of this literature to our people.

Again the preacher is set to instruct and inspire the one organization to which our times must increasingly look for the defense, the preservation of the Christian Sabbath. The state can establish a holiday, but cannot establish a holy day, a day of re-creation, from which a man may, as one puts it, approach a new week of work " with a clearer, happier sense of God and duty." Often you have been reminded of the forces which are breaking down our Sabbath, the forces of " the money-makers and the merry-makers." The Sabbath is to-day what it was in the days of Emerson, " the core of our civilization, the jubilee of the whole world." It is God's great gift of love to tired people.

Still further the preacher ministers to our times, as he instructs and inspires the organization which by its history and constitution seeks the sanctity of the home. Our

faith was born in a home which found shelter
for the time in the stable of the inn of Beth-
lehem.   In the upper room of a private house
the Master and His disciples gathered for the
last supper.   In the upper room of a private
house the infant Church was born.   There was
a church in the house of Philemon, another
church in the house of Priscilla and Aquila.
In times of persecution, the Church has always
fled for refuge to the home.   There have been
times when the cloister and the hearth were
supposed to be on different levels of religious
life.   In the thought of Jesus the cloister sur-
rounds and shelters the hearth, and in that
cloister walk father and mother, and children's
voices mingle with theirs, and the hearth itself
becomes an altar.   "The whole effort of Jesus
on its human side," says Matheson, "is to
make the world a cosmopolitan home.   .   .   .
There should be no going out from the family
circle into the world ; there should be a bring-
ing of the world into the family circle."   To-
day the pressure of population and of poverty,
the factory system which separates a man
from his tools, the crimes of the pleasure
seeker, the popular lack of ideals are all
working for the destruction of the home.
But Professor Peabody, the teacher of us all,
has truly said : "The home holds the key to
the salvation of the state."   I look without

hope to any other institution than the Church to save to us the home. The Church must and can do it.

To speak more largely : the preacher is set to instruct and inspire the organization which beyond all others is commissioned and equipped to keep the soul of our country alive. A German has divided his countrymen into Soul-Germans and Stomach-Germans. There are soul-Americans, and then there are stomach-Americans. How can the soul of our country be kept alive except by the multiplication of soul-Americans, Americans whose souls are alive to God ? The task is not small. Swiftly the conditions change. In a single spring time, 200,000 people move into the single state of North Dakota. Graham Taylor calls our attention to the Frontier in the Rear, the crowded tenement sections of our great cities. Thirty solid blocks, for example, in New York fill up with Italians. The task is not small, but it is supremely the task of the Church, backed, led by the Christian preacher, to keep the soul of our country alive. "Let it never be forgotten," says Silvester Horne, " that modern America sprang out of the ideal relation between a pastor and a church, a man of God and a people of God."

But if the preacher helps to keep the soul

of America alive, he is doing much to quicken the faltering, dying souls of other lands. Your business men are familiar with the exceeding mobility of our foreign population. With every winter, and especially with every time of financial stringency multitudes of our immigrants have been accustomed to pass through the outward swinging gates of our republic. I noticed that on a December day of a recent year, the steamer *President Lincoln* set sail from New York for Naples, carrying 3,600 Italians. What did those Italians know about Lincoln's country? How much did they know of Lincoln's God, Lincoln's Bible, Lincoln's loving human brotherhood? It is estimated that at the close of the war, 500,000 of our foreign born may return to their native lands. These missionaries to broken-hearted Europe, these men who go at their own charges, who know the vernacular of speech and of thought, understand the prejudices and presuppositions of their listeners, these men who understand the psychological climates of their countries, these men it is the preacher's function, directly or indirectly, to touch with the life of God, and through them to quicken the souls of their own lands, the soul of Europe.

And this leads me to say that the preacher ministers to our times, as he instructs and inspires the one organization which must finance and man that enterprise which Mackenzie the historian declares to be foremost of those enterprises which are destined to transform the face of the world. I refer to the enterprise of foreign missions. You may ask your Jewish philanthropist to build your hospitals for America. In many a non-Christian land, the Church must build them. You may ask your infidel brother, with more or less hope of response, to care for the blind, the deaf, the hunger-bitten and the leprous of America. The burden of this work in many a non-Christian land falls upon the Church at home. Who will send forth God's missionaries to thwart the devil's missionaries over there? Who will send forth ambassadors of the religion of love who shall avert or allay the friction which always arises when West meets East? Who will send forth interpreters of Jesus who shall undo the infernal work of misinterpretation wrought by the great war? Who will carry the evangel to individuals whose religion has brought to them only bad news? Sacrificial as they are, the Christians of Europe for a generation will be hamstrung in their efforts at world-evangelization. For a generation almost exclusively, for the generations very largely, the burden of the Christianization of the world will rest upon the organization which the American preacher is set to instruct and to inspire. The words of John Ruskin have lost none of their meaning : " The issues of life and death for modern society are in the pulpit."

Better than any other man, in a fashion absolutely unique, the preacher is enabled to turn the life of our times from its discontents and failures to Him who is the only source of satisfaction, to present to men the personality which alone meets and responds to the aspirations, the emphasis, the appreciations of our times. The times are on tiptoe to greet the preacher, always provided the preacher is the right kind of man.

What kind of man must the preacher be, if he is to be the preacher for the times? In the finest sense of the term he must be a man of the world. His life must thrill with the life of his times. By the experience of his own heart or by spiritual imagination, he must understand the discontents and failures, the aspirations, the emphasis, the appreciations. As Schauffler suggests, he must be more familiar with the church sons than the church fathers, better acquainted with Jim and Sam than with Origen and Chrysostom —*whom by the way he ought to know*. He must be the voice of the inarticulate multitude, saying what the multitude longs to say, but cannot. After all there must be a difference. The clerical garb is a symbol, rather pathetic symbol perhaps, of a separateness which ought to exist between the preacher and the world. The preacher while a man of the world must be God's man. As God's man, he must hold or rather be held by certain great convictions. When the Congregationalists of Japan were revising their creed, one Japanese preacher said, " I would put into my creed only those convictions for which I should be willing to die." Whatever may be the penumbral beliefs of the preacher's study, the preacher in his pulpit must be conquered by certain convictions for which he would gladly die, yes, for which he would gladly let his loved ones die. It is a good thing for a man occasionally to face this question : " For how many of the beliefs I uttered last Sabbath should I be willing to die? Nay, in imagination I will stand, as many of my brothers have stood, prisoner on the bloody floor of a Chinese yamen. There I will face this alternative : Give up the belief you preached last Sunday, or your little child will be killed before your eyes, your wife will be tortured and killed before your eyes, and then you will be tortured and killed." Some beliefs that have seemed central, fundamental, will slip silently away to climb your study stairs, to rest undisturbed upon the top of your Hebrew Bible. Other convictions will come forth naked, unashamed, living, glorious, conquering.

This means of course that the preacher for our times must be a man of courage. He must be able to enter into the experience of Frederick Robertson, who says, "Once in my life I knew and I rejoiced to know that I was pronouncing the sentence of a coward's and a liar's hell." The preacher may not be one of Dawson's "tame prophets bound with chains of gold." No slave can preach. He must have a prophet's heroism, take the prophet's risk, be "a hero for the invisible," glad to know that

> "Life may be given in many ways,
> And loyalty to Truth be sealed
> As bravely in the closet as the field."

As God's man, the preacher for our times must be a man of divine compassion. We have read somewhere of a man who had only so good a heart as could be made out of brains. God has no work for that man in the pulpit. I delight in that story told of Beecher. He was asked, "Mr. Beecher, what is the feeling dominant in your heart as you face your vast audience?" He replied, "Compassion, Compassion." Most of us, as we face our audiences, are filled with our sermons or our fears. As Jesus faced the five thousand on the grassy slopes of the Lake of Galilee, He was moved with compassion. The Puritan preacher remembered that Jerusalem had sinned, and he poured out his woes upon her guilty life. The preacher for our times remembers the sin, oh yes, but he also remembers the banishment and the bondage, the harps hanging on the willows, the silenced songs of the exile ; and he speaks comfortably straight to the heart of Jerusalem.

Again, as God's man, God's devotee, the preacher for our times will know in his heart and express in his words the joy of the soldier who marches on to victory. What was it that made the sad old world listen to the first message of Christianity ? It was the joy of the Christians. What gives power to some of the newer sects with their feeble elephant-breath philosophies ? It is their note of victorious joy. As the average preacher stands in his pulpit, you ask yourself involuntarily, "Who's dead ? " or you sigh, "There must be whooping cough again at the parsonage." Just think of that man Paul. Beaten and imprisoned in Philippi, hurried secretly out of Thessalonica, driven from Berœa, laughed out of Athens, in Corinth haled before the judgment seat of

Gallio, everywhere bonds and afflictions
abide him . . . yet he cries jubilantly,
" Thanks be to God who always leadeth us in
the triumph train of Christ and by us as censer
bearers sheddeth abroad the fragrance of the
knowledge of him in every place throughout the world." May not the preacher have
the glorious morning face of the man who
has achieved "the eternal worth while"?

We hear a brother preacher reply to all
this: " You don't know my field, its sceptics
and critics and cynics and dyspeptics." No
I don't. But I know other fields. I got a
letter a while ago from one of our graduates :
" The church was organized with thirteen
members, and by October of the next year it
had grown to eighteen. Of these, three of
the charter members never really came to
church. Three more of the charter list and
two of the others had left town, and two
others had withdrawn to assist in starting a
' Christian' church. Of the eight who re-
mained in good standing, three are half-
hearted in their support of the church." No,
I don't know your church; but I remember
a certain monk by the name of Luther who
began to preach to his times in a little room
twenty by thirty feet. I have heard of a
certain tinker of pots and kettles and pans,
who walked through the muddy streets of

Elstow, or lay in the foul prison of Bedford, yet sojourned in the Palace Beautiful, walked the heights of the Delectable Mountains, made his way by the gates into the city. I have read that Charles Kingsley "spent his whole life in a little patch of moorland, a parish with but seven or eight hundred people, not one of whom when he began his ministry could read or write." We have heard of the man who said, "My garden is very small, but oh, it is wondrous high," and I think that there is no man who tills a garden so small, but that it reaches up and up to the suburbs of Paradise.

That is a fine word of the Chronicler: "From day to day men came to David to help him, until there was a host like unto the host of God." So I see them coming. To the man of the world, who with David has tasted the deep experiences of humanity, to God's man, convinced, courageous, compassionate, joyous, I see them coming. Coming to hear him preach? I do not say that. I see them coming, to catch the inspiration of the message of his life—I see them coming, until there gathers about that man a host like unto the host of God.

The great days of preaching are coming back. Only let us go forth to meet them and to greet them as they come.

II

The Preacher and His Sermon

II

THE PREACHER AND HIS SERMON

AS a prelude to our discussion, I would say a few words regarding the minister's wife. In this prelude there are "three heads, all small, bald," but we trust not quite "empty." First, the minister's wife and the congregation; Second, the minister's wife and her children; Third, the minister's wife and her husband.

First and least important: The minister's wife and the congregation. The minister's wife will learn to keep silence in seven languages. Has her husband worked pretty hard for a week? She will not refer to the fact. Has her husband a poorly prepared sermon? She will not go around telling how the dear man has had nervous indigestion all the week. She knows everything about the congregation, but in the ladies' meetings she knows nothing. A gossip comes and pours forth some tale of some son of worthlessness, and she replies, "Is that so? By the way, don't you think that the new Boys' Scout troop is just fine?"

She will learn not only to keep silence;

she will learn also to refuse election to office. If there is another woman in the congregation, that woman must be the president of the Women's Society. The minister's wife may encourage, soothe, direct, but never lead. Her best work is done by writing letters, by calling quietly upon the sick, by helping the mothers and their little ones. I know such a woman. She couldn't speak in meeting if she were given as reward a trip to Europe in peace times. But she has a way of slipping into a sick room. She puts a bunch of carnations on the table beside the sick woman, and smoothes the pillow a little, and leaves in the room the radiant sunshine of her love. She takes to her home Mrs. Jones's three older children while little Johnnie has the measles. Now this is not advertised in the *Oscaloosa Thunderer*, but it is noticed in heaven, whence she came.

Second: The minister's wife and her children. The minister's wife will do her best to see that her children do not disgrace the minister and the church. This task is not so easy as at first it might appear. Every minister's small son is supposed to be an ensample to the flock. Any well organized boy hates to be pointed out as the minister's son, and he may be tempted to go far to effect a disguise. The mother moreover will do her best to see that her children do not acquire a perfect abhorrence of the ministry, of the church and of religion.   Are Mrs. J's eccentricities accentuated at the family table?   Is Deacon S's stinginess dwelt upon?   Is Pastor Q's wiliness the main topic of conversation?   The small boy will determine within his little soul, "By all the clergymen in the United States, I will never be one."

Third: The minister's wife and her husband.   The minister's wife will love her husband, but she will not coddle him.   She will compel her husband to pay his bills to the butcher, the baker, the candlestick maker, and to pay them at the first of the month, if he does not pay at the time of purchase. She will probably insist that the minister give her a stated allowance, with which she may do the buying for the family.   If the minister claims that he has no money at the beginning of the month, the wife will tell him that it is simply because of the ragged, wretched system of church support which he has introduced or tolerated.   Loving her husband, but not coddling him, she will compel him to tear up all letters emanating from firms which long to sell him oil stock, gold mines, and the like.   These firms spend vast sums of money upon us ministers, knowing that of all men on earth we have the least *common* sense.

The minister's wife will compel her husband to be a law-abiding citizen. He has no more right to run across the grass in front of the church than has the member of the infant class. He has no right to run in upon Mrs. Nomaid, when she is preparing supper. These things the wife will show to her husband, who half unconsciously considers himself like Napoleon above all law. The minister's wife will compel her husband to be cleanly in his person. I know a prominent minister who damages his influence unspeakably because his coat is not clean, his face is not clean, his hair is not cut. The minister is an absent-minded beggar. When his mind is absent, his wife must lend him hers.

Loving her husband, but refusing to coddle him, the minister's wife will compel him to work and to work hard. She will insist that her husband be in his office at eight A. M. If possible his office should be in the church and not at home, so that the people of the town will see that he goes to work as they go to work. Not only that: she must insist that her husband study when he is in his study. To read the newspapers is not to study. To read the average magazine is not to study. She will see that he stays in his study from eight A. M. to twelve M. and *studies.* No chickens in the back yard, no children in the front yard, no vegetables going to waste in the garden, can ever excuse him from working at his job.

Again, this minister's wife will insist that no sweetness and light, no pastoral calls upon the halt, the lame, the blind; no funerals, no weddings, no Y. P. S. C. E. addresses, no temperance lectures, can ever take the place of his preaching. No hurried preparation at two o'clock Sunday morning, no reference to Henry Ward Beecher's preparation after Sunday breakfast, will excuse this man from the most careful pulpit preparation. He is a preacher. He must "begin, continue, close the work for which he draws the wage."

On Sunday afternoon, the minister's wife will make a few notes on the morning sermon. To these she will not allude on Sunday. In the evening as she loves her husband and pities him she will be allowed to stroke his head, to hold his hand; but Monday, rather, Tuesday morning, she will come to his study and tell him the truth. She will frankly say to him, "My dear, I have heard many poor sermons in my life, but none quite so bad as Sunday's." Nor will that suffice. She must tell him why and how it was bad. "The matter was badly arranged, and there wasn't much matter to be arranged. Your delivery was execrable. You have a curious way of holding wildly to your pulpit as to a life raft." Loving her husband truly and intelligently she gradually transforms him into a real minister.

The minister's wife does not have as many new hats as her classmate. The dress in which she graduated from college must appear at the high school commencements of her parish for many years. She wears the crown of a people's peculiar personal affection, and the angels toil day after day upon the fabric of the new robe which she will never have to change or turn.

I must omit a prelude which I should like to give, entitled, The Preacher and his Sexton. Each man of us doubtless has suffered many things from many sextons. For example, there is the sexton who thinks that he has done the whole duty of a sexton when he has heated his building so that no creature but a salamander could escape suffocation. There is the sexton who on a cold winter morning decides to take care of his fires fifteen minutes before service. Henry Ward Beecher tells us that in his first church he was his own sexton. I have often thought that this was one reason for his early success as a preacher. I would defy Beecher himself to keep his audience awake when preaching in the atmosphere to which a sexton will now and again subject the congregation. There is a sexton who shall be nameless, for I know that many of you would immediately offer him a salary larger than he is getting. He does not overheat or underheat his building. He does not shake the furnace when you are in the midst of the pastoral prayer. He does not open the windows at the most important point in the sermon. Like a good usher and a virtuous woman, his price is above rubies. The good sexton is the silent but indispensable partner of the good preacher.

Shall we consider now the immediate subject in hand ? We have all sat at the feet of great preachers, and have heard them praise our calling. We have heard Dr. Forsyth remark, " I will venture to say that with its preaching Christianity stands or falls," and we have said, " Amen." We have heard Dr. Jefferson say, " Preaching is your highest business. Nothing can ever take its place. You are to be administrators, but administration will not take the place of preaching. Unless you are preachers, you are not likely to have much to administer." And again we have said, " Amen." We have heard the short ugly word of Dr. Brown before the English Baptist Union: "A minister must be able to preach." And again we have said, "Amen." Indeed there is no man of us who does not offer daily the worthy prayer, "O God, make me a good preacher." And yet as we face a new Sabbath, we face, each of us, a new pile of glittering white paper, each sheet of which seems to jeer: "You know very well you can't preach. You never could preach, you never will preach. You haven't one new thing to say next Sunday." Can we help each other? The thought of "Ecce Homo" cheers one: "While the prophet whose prophecy is new in substance is no prophet, so the prophet whose prophecy is old in form is no prophet but a plagiarist."

As preachers, speakers for God, we do not for an instant claim that the substance of our message from Sabbath to Sabbath is new. Rather we glory in the fact that our task has been, is and always will be the same; to bring every thought of men into captivity to the obedience of the God who reveals Himself in Jesus Christ.

"Subtlest thought shall fail and learning falter,
   Churches change, forms perish, systems go,
   But our human needs, they will not alter,
   Christ no after age shall e'er outgrow."

If by God's grace we can only preach Christ, so that men shall see Him, we shall have fulfilled our highest, our sole ambition.

The substance of the message is not new; on the other hand, the prophet whose prophecy is old in form is no prophet but a plagiarist.

How then shall we gain the novelty of sermonic form, which the prophecy of to-day requires? Or to state our question more broadly and truly, How may we hope to prepare and preach sermons to our times?

We shall read books, not widely perhaps, but well. We have all made note of the retirement of Dr. Clifford from his London church after a continuous pastorate of fifty-seven years. See what he says of his reading: "I believe in keeping a good biography on hand for stimulus, encouragement and inspiration. The second kind of reading is what I would call disciplinary. It is reading with the deliberate purpose of keeping the machine in order, of keeping one's mental knife edge as keen as possible. Such hard, stiff reading is a *sine qua non* for the preacher who would protect his mind against the cheapening, shallowing process which operates upon every man who does not in some real sense remain a student all his days. The third type of reading is the explicitly professional, the reading definitely for next Sunday's sermon." Benson as well as Clifford emphasizes the importance of biography, and suggests that we should read especially the lives of great contemporaries. These men are the fruits of the past and the roots of the age that is to be. Some preachers read many sermons of other men. Most of us would find the burden laid upon us greater than we could bear. But some sermons are stimulating. In reading a sermon, one finds it interesting to get at the processes by which a great preacher works his way into and out of his subject. What led him to think of this idea? How did he proceed to that next idea? Innocent but inquisitive Delilahs, we shall compel this Samson of a preacher to tell us wherein his great strength lieth.

As we study the printed page, we shall be students of nature. What a curious fact is that, noted by Nash, that while Calvin lived long by Lake Geneva, there is no evidence that he ever really saw it.

As we study books and nature we shall study men, men who are now upon the earth. Here for example is the man in the pew. In one of his annual reports, Dr. Pritchett says, "A hundred years ago ministers were the educated men of their communities, and their power was in proportion. In the interval, the congregations have risen enormously in the scale of general education. With this rise, the law and medicine have to a large extent kept pace, but the Church has relatively fallen back. In the Protestant churches where the power of authority has largely passed away, the Church depends upon the quality of the religious leadership of its preachers. The efficiency in this leadership is low." Study then the man in the pew. You discover that your message is not heard simply because it is the message of the Church or of the preacher. Your judgment is weighed, and not seldom found wanting. "You sit in your tower study all the week and then come down to censor us, who have been bearing the burden of the day and the scorching heat."

But you follow this "man in the pew" to his home. Once in a while you hear a very great preacher or a very small theologue disparage pastoral calls. He will not be bothered by pink tea visitations. You go to the hospital to sit beside a young fellow who, in order that his mother at his death may have his insurance money, has attempted to commit suicide. Is that pink tea visitation? You call upon an aged woman who is about to slip out into the other world, you

repeat to her the old words, "He that be-
lieveth on me, though he were dead, yet
shall he live, and whosoever liveth and be-
lieveth on me shall never die." You talk
with a Sunday-school teacher about the best
way to handle a large class of small boys.
You take the hand of a father whose daughter has gone wrong. Is that pink tea visitation?

I suppose one of the most impressive
preachers in New York is Dr. Jowett. I do
not know how much calling he does, but
these words of his are significant: "When I
have got my theme clearly defined, and I begin to prepare its exposition, I keep in the
circle of my mind a dozen men and women
very varied in their natural temperaments
and very dissimilar in their daily circumstances. These are not mere abstractions.
Neither are they dolls and dummies. They
are real men and women whom I know, professional people, trading people, learned and
ignorant, rich and poor. When I am preparing my work, my mind is constantly
glancing round this invisible circle, and I consider how I can so serve the bread of this
particular truth as to provide welcome nutri-
ment for all. What relation has this teaching to that barrister? How can the truth be
related to that doctor? What have I here

for that keenly nervous woman with the artistic temperament? And there is that poor body, upon whom the floods of sorrow have been rolling their billows for many years. What of her? And so on, all round the circle." Perhaps a man can do that kind of sermon preparation without pastoral calling. Could you? When John Mitchell was asked, "What courses of study would you introduce into the seminary?" he replied, "Several courses in human sympathy." Speaking of Charles Brown, of England, one writes: "He belongs to the happily once more increasing class to whom pastoral visitation is a holy ministry. One could not picture him like a very eloquent preacher it was my misfortune to know, writing to one of his regular members three months after his death."

Nor will the preacher confine his studies of men to the man in the pew; he will study as well the greatly overworked man in the street, the man who finds utterance in the lodge rooms, in the labour conclaves of the country, in the secular press. "What good came of it at last?" The sensible question of little Peterkin is being asked insistently. The man in the street sees splendid church edifices, discovers the preachers apparently neither among the toilers nor the spinners. He marks the remission of taxes on church property, and the correspondingly increased taxation upon other property. He measures achievements by the yard-stick of his own business. You may recall an editorial in the *Springfield Republican* a while ago: " Next Sunday the churches of the city of Springfield will be opened after the summer vacation. It will now be their task to show the people of this city if they are worth the expense involved in opening and maintaining them."

Bishop Spaulding of Utah, that gallant young knight whose sudden death we lament, said to us men in Oberlin: "There is no man who can cut down through so many strata of society as the minister." Let us cut down.

A student of all sorts and conditions of men, the preacher will be as well a student of movements of thought and organization. Here are religious enterprises outside the pale of Protestant orthodoxy, enterprises which appeal to numbers of well dressed and supposedly intelligent people, whose devotion to their creed and church puts us all to shame, who point with perfect confidence to the fruits of their faith to validate their creeds. Such enterprises deserve reflection rather than ridicule. The study of movements will involve the more hopeful and profitable study of the Federal Council of Churches, the League to

Enforce Peace, the World Alliance of the
Churches for the Promotion of International
Friendship. A student need not be an expert. But only by such study can we escape
the sharp stab of the epigram of Voltaire,
quoted by Vedder, "Medicine is the art of
putting drugs of which we know little into
bodies of which we know less, to cure diseases
of which we know nothing at all." Isn't
that a charming suggestion: "A preacher
should have in his study one mirror but
many windows"?

Now all this sympathetic study of ours re-
lates itself more or less consciously to the
main task of life. There are few more pathetic
sights about a college campus than the sight
of a man who has gone on studying, studying, adding initials to his name, only that
and nothing more. The student is the free
servant of the preacher. The minister must
be able to preach.

"Well," you say, "while you have been
indulging in these glittering generalities,
that pile of glittering white paper has been
staring at me, jeering at me. What of my
particular Sunday sermon?" Perhaps that
question was or ought to have been decided
last summer when you were thinking through
your plan of campaign for the ensuing year.
In the summer you labelled great envelopes

or folders with such titles as Communion, Thanksgiving, Foreign Missions, New Years. As a non-ritualist, you have found special delight in planning for the large use of the days of the Christian Year. It is one of the ways in which we may emphasize our fellowship with multitudes of our brethren in the Christian Church throughout the world. You have of course marked certain folders, Christmas, Palm Sunday, Easter. Perhaps you have decided to observe such days as Epiphany, Whitsunday, Ascension Day. You have always found it particularly hard to preach on the evening of a great feast day. You were glad to notice that the observance of the Christian year suggests the 26th of December as St. Stephen's Day, the day commemorating the man who better than any of his contemporaries to date understood the implications of the message of Jesus.

Again, last summer you labelled certain folders with the names of the days of patriotism. You determined in some fashion to mark Forefathers' Day, Lincoln's Birthday, Washington's Birthday. A discriminating Englishman said to me that a serious calamity to England at the present crisis is the long failure of England to teach patriotism to her industrial classes.

Last summer too, you determined that this year you would observe at least by some pulpit reference, in the morning or the evening, certain days of reform, like Prison Sunday, Universal Peace Sunday. You made tentative plans for the suitable celebration, in the fall, of Covenant Sunday, when you would speak particularly to the parents and teachers of the Bible School pupils. You thought a little way into a special service and sermon for Children's Day. Not that you decided to make of yourself a talking almanac, but that you did decide to meet in a sympathetic and helpful way the mood and temper of your people and your community. As you were considering your plan of campaign for the church year, you thought at or through certain plans for the evening services. There were to be brief courses of consecutive sermons. Or you decided that on the first Sunday of each of four months you would preach an expository sermon on one of the parables, on the second Sunday you would make a preacher's study of some great biography, on the third Sunday you would consider some aspect of social or civic reform, on the last Sunday you would preach an evangelistic sermon.

Thus the labelled folders began to multiply; but you remind me of that busy woman who in an attempt to catch up with her correspondence found much comfort in addressing and stamping envelopes, which she never filled. A labelled envelope is not a sermon. That is true, but it is also true that thoughts fly to labelled envelopes as doves fly to their windows.

In those summer days moreover you decided what should be the special emphasis of your work for the new church year. Perhaps you said nothing about this to any one; but you determined to emphasize definite and persistent Bible study, or some aspect of world evangelism, or individual work for individuals, or the reconstruction of the business and social life of your community in accordance with the teachings of Jesus. This decision has helped to dictate not alone your reading but your choice of the year's sermon material.

But alas, how can a man give novelty of form to one hundred and four sermons dealing with the same old substance of thought? The task is not light, but it is not impossible. In obedience to a suggestion of George Adam Smith, you were giving some months of study to the book of Deuteronomy. You were not getting along very well, but at last came to this passage, " The eternal God is thy dwelling-place, and underneath are the ever-

lasting arms"; and you saw the Jerusalem of
Josiah's day, ground as wheat beneath the
upper and the nether millstones of Assyrian
and Egyptian policies, busy politicians hurry-
ing hither and yon to find some new master to
serve, an ignorant populace climbing to the
house roofs to discover some new gods to
worship, a young king with more zeal than
wisdom trying to reform Jehovah worship. A
book is discovered in the debris of the temple.
As it is read to the king it approves itself to be
the law of God. As the king hears, he rends
his garments and weeps, but at the last of
the book the great words come to his ears,
"The eternal God is thy dwelling-place, and
underneath are the everlasting arms." " O
King, no king's palace is thy dwelling-place,
the eternal God is thy home. No arms of
flesh sustain thee; underneath are the everlasting arms." You have your sermon. All
that home means, when it means most, Life,
Love, Rest, Joy, that and more God means.
That and more. Why more? Because God
is God, and one marks the emphasis upon
that word Eternal. "The eternal God is thy
home." We are like the children of a king
who on the palace floor build their little
shacks. Let them tear down the shacks,
they will find themselves in the palace.
Again, "Underneath are the everlasting

arms." All that a father's arms mean when they mean most, that and more God's support must mean. What do a father's arms mean? Protection, Peace, Strength. We remember seeing a little baby placed in his older brother's arms. The baby cried for fright. The baby did not realize that both he and his brother were in the strong arms of the mother. Underneath, away down underneath, are the everlasting arms. So your sermon grows in your folder sermon garden.

Or again, in your reading of the New Testament, you happened upon Dr. Moffatt's literal translation, and there flashed upon you the words, "We are a colony of heaven." How beautiful! . . . and all your fading memories of the rights and obligations of the Roman colony came to your mind, and another sermon began to grow.

You chanced to be reading a sermon of Campbell, and you came upon words like these, "As I was climbing a mountain one misty morning, I saw what I took to be a monster. As I drew nearer I saw it was a man. As I met him I saw he was my brother." And by some association of ideas, there came to you, without your seeking, the great words, "The dayspring from on high shall visit us, to shine upon them that sit in darkness and the shadow of death, to guide our feet into the way of peace." "Illumination, Guidance." With the coming of the day-dawn, men who have groped about in the half light seeing monster shapes now find the pathway to peace, and in every man see their brother.

One evening you were reading Mrs. Browning's "Casa Guidi Windows." You came upon these lines:

" So rise up henceforth with a cheerful smile,
    And having strewn the violets, reap the corn,
    And having reaped and garnered, bring the plough,
    And draw new furrows 'neath the healthy morn,
    And plant the great Hereafter in this Now."

The thought gripped you: "Planting the great Hereafter in this Now." As you knelt in prayer that night, it held you still: "Planting the great Hereafter in this Now." The next morning you woke with the idea which would not let you go. You didn't read Mrs. Browning to get a sermon; but as an additional largess, she gave you the germ of one which would grow in your sermon garden.

You were glancing over an *Atlantic Monthly:* "The writer knows a young Frenchman who when the war broke out had lived for three years in this country, and hoped to make it a permanent home. To him his mother wrote, 'My son, your two

brothers are at the front. Are you not coming back to fight for France?'" Are you
not coming back to fight for—for what? for
France? Will a man leave comfort, peace,
life, and lay them all a willing sacrifice on the
altar of patriotism, and shall we not find
Americans who will answer the summons of
the Kingdom? So you thought, not in order
to preach. So you thought because you
were a preacher. And your seed was planted
which one day would become a sermon on
The Call of the Kingdom.

Or you noticed a news item: "Now in
preparation for another raid this winter, the
Turks have built a temporary railroad, con-
necting with the Damascus Haifa line down
through Nablus and Lydda to Beersheba.
They have torn up the tracks from Jaffa as
far as Lydda but retain the Jerusalem con-
nection." The little item was just the needed
spark to set your mind aflame to start a
series of sermons which should deal with
certain other travellers along those ancient
paths, or perhaps with the problems of the
Life and Leaders of the Early Church.

So, now it is a Bible passage that yields
you your sermon germ, now it is a narrative
from the common life, now a poem, now a
letter, now the careful consideration of some
theme of theology. The infinite riches of life,

of all life, are ours.   Dr. Jefferson has some
delightful remarks to this effect: " It is not
well to cultivate the homiletic habit, the
habit of demanding a pound of sermonic
flesh from every Antonio you chance to
meet.   One ought not to be thinking shop
all the time.   A man who is always working
for sermons is as foolish as a man who is
always working for money.   Landscapes and
historic ruins and children, and all other
lovely things are to be enjoyed.   We wrong
a book when we read it simply for the things
which we can use.   It is desecration of a
poem to read it for fine phrases with which
to deck a sermon, and we wrong the master-
piece of an historian if we follow him only
for an illustration with which to brighten up
an argument.   It is only when we gloriously
forget ourselves, as Mrs. Browning has reminded us, and plunge headlong into the
depths of the author's thought that we get
out of a book the best thing which the book
has to give."

We may accept the teaching of the para-
graph, while remembering at the same time
certain facts: A preacher may not read a
poem in order to find a sermon, but as he
reads he does not cease to be a preacher.   I
have been interested to sit behind a con-
servatory professor during the concert of

some great musician who plays the instrument which the professor teaches. The professor's body sways back and forth with the rhythm of the music. Indeed his nervous system seems to be a harp on which the musician plays, and yet on the morrow the professor will point out to his pupils the accuracy or the defects of the artist's technique, will analyze with merciless fidelity the elements of the master's art. In listening to the concert, the professor does not cease to be a professor. The homiletic faculty, if you please, does not sleep when the faculty of appreciation is most awake. When Jowett made a little toy water-wheel for his child, and used the waters of the Welsh hills to drive the wheel, he did not help his child in order to preach, but his task lost none of its fascination, as he was led by it to think as a preacher that a man may get the great river of God's life and power to operate the little mill of his personal life, as his task reminded him of the text, "The Lord is MY Strength." Speaking to the younger men in the ministry, I should dare to go even further, and to remind them that Bushnell "cultivated determinately the preacher's habit of mind." It is instructive to study the biographer's excerpts from Phillips Brooks's early notebooks, and to see how the man was making his reading, his experiences, his observations serve his preaching. One who has dealt at all with seminary students will bear me out in saying that while in their college courses they have been walking over acres of homiletical diamonds, they come into the seminary utterly unaware of their wealth. The homiletic habit is not a disastrous habit for a young man to cultivate provided it does not become a monomania. Walking is easy when you know how to walk. The homiletic habit does not need to be cultivated, when you have it, and the reason is that the habit persists and flourishes without assistance

Still that Sunday sermon goes unwatched, untended. What about it? I think I can see a sickly little sprout sticking its head above the ground. Let us try to cultivate it. "But I don't feel like preparing a sermon this morning." That doesn't make any difference. We shall do everything within our power to make ourselves feel like working. You remember that James suggests: "Compared with what we ought to be, we are half awake. Our fires are damped, our drafts are checked. We are making use of only a small part of our possible mental and physical resources."

I heard of one man, who when he felt

"like a walrus on an ice floe, heavy, melancholy, ineffective," could warm and vitalize and make efficient his powers if he put on a dress-suit, and went to his desk as to a dance. A friend of mine has a victrola, which by request will play for him a Beethoven sonata, and lift him up into the seventh heaven, where he hears unspeakable words which it is not lawful for a man to utter. The experience however gives him words to speak to his congregation. The winds of heaven may not always blow upon a man's sails, but the sails must be ready to catch them when they come. You have read the word of Philo, "At times, coming to my work empty I have suddenly become full, ideas being sown upon me in showers from above." We have all tasted of that divine experience. Eight hours' sleep, a light breakfast, a quiet sunny room for uninterrupted study, a room which as one suggests is not so much an office as an oratory,—these for most preachers are essentials. Have you ever ventured into the workshop of a poor preacher? It reminds you of the anteroom of a children's nursery, or the vestibule of the morgue. All is explained, the cluttered sermon, the chilling sermon, the dead sermon.

Let us then assume that the external conditions of study are favourable. Let us as-

sume that we have our text. Deliberately
we study it. Then with great care we study
the context. In case of doubt as to exegesis,
we dig into an International Critical Commentary, provided the correct volume has
come from the press. I am planning to will
to my descendants my order for the complete
set, which I executed a decade ago. If the
International Commentary is not available,
we shall use some other commentary which
compels us to think rather than permits us
to stop thinking. There are great names
subscribed to letters commending homiletical commentaries which would make a man
a mental Mephibosheth for life. No preacher
ever thrived on peptonized food.

Gradually out of the gloom our theme ap-
pears, the thing we are going to preach about,
the sermon in little. Perhaps it chances to
develop into a straight ethical sermon. How
is a man going to be saved from saying an
undisputed thing in such a solemn way?
Has not a writer said, "Men see already with
exasperating clearness what their duty is"?
Yes, they do, sometimes. Sometimes a man
will say to you quite plainly as a man said
a while ago to Rauschenbusch, "I cannot be
a Christian; there is too much lying in my
business." To men who see their duty with
exasperating clearness, our message is the

message of the cross. And at a time when ninety-five per cent. of Europe's university men have been sent to the front, and the greater part destroyed, I will not believe that the men of America will refuse the call of the cross. Will Jesus not find men in the industrial life of America who will dare to be Christians? Jesus has found them, will find them.

> "And where is the man who comes up from the throng,
> Who does the new deed, and who sings the new song,
> And who makes the old world as a world that is new?
> And who is the man? It is you! it is you!
> And our praise is exultant and proud.
> We are waiting for you there, for you are the man!
> Come up from the jostle as soon us you can;
> Come up from the crowd there, for you are the man,—
> The man who comes up from the crowd."

But there are hosts of men who do not see their duty clearly, who would like to do their duty if they knew it. Your ethical sermon will help these men to find the narrow but divinely wide gate that leads into Jesus' way. And as you prepare your sermon you will find courage for your task in the words of Faunce: "There is more eagerness to hear a worthy appeal to the sense of duty to-day than ever since Miles Standish stepped on Plymouth Rock."

Or your sermon turns out to be a strictly doctrinal sermon. We have hesitated to preach sermons dealing with doctrine, but I ask you men who have been preaching the past years what sermons have met the most immediate, obvious and hearty response. I venture to believe they have been sermons in which you have spoken of the God we trust, the Master we serve, the Eternal Life. President Eliot truly says: "Through constant changes in direction of interests, theological themes remain the themes of supreme interest to thinking men." But can we put the ancient message of doctrine into new forms? Not only can we do so. We must do so. You know men, I doubt not, in your very seminary, men who know all the old arguments, who are fighting in half despair for their faith in the personality of God, the supremacy of Christ, the reality of the Eternal Life. Only this week it may be you received a letter from a man of choicest spirit who sees no other hope for the after-death than that of "the choir invisible, of those immortal dead, who live again,"—who live alone—"in lives made better by their presence." The preparation of your doctrinal sermon becomes not a cloister study in theology. It is the preparation of food for starving men, it is the launching of a life-boat for wrestlers with the troubled sea.

Or your sermon turns out to be an experimental sermon, and deals with the deep experiences of your people, their sorrows, their fears, their joys. Learning does not help a man whose reputation has been ruined. Education does not uphold a woman whose heart has been crushed by the death of her little daughter. You remember that fine word regarding Dr. Watson: "He had a great eye for the sunrise"; and that personal word of his, "Never can I forget what a distinguished scholar who used to sit in my church once said to me, 'Your best work has been to put heart into men for the coming week.'" Our dean told me that his baby daughter used to sleep in a crib beside the father's bed, and sometimes in the darkness of the midnight, the father would hear the baby's voice: "Hand, Hand," and when the father's hand was upon her own she was at rest. Your experimental sermon as it develops in your study is no mere affair of homiletics. It is a great loving effort to put heart into men for the coming week, to make men conscious of the hand which presses strong and tender upon the hand of each bewildered child of God.

But it is most probable that you will not be able very glibly to identify your sermon as ethical or doctrinal or experimental. Your ethics passes into doctrine, your doctrine into ethics, and both into Christian experience. Dr. Fosdick calls attention to the words of George MacDonald in his "Robert Falconer," "This is a sane, wholesome, practical working faith, first, that it is a man's business to do the will of God, second, that God takes on Himself the special care of that man, and third, that therefore that man ought never to be afraid of anything." In the enunciation of that wholesome practical working faith, we shall emphasize now the ethical, now the doctrinal, now the experimental aspect.

As you sit at your desk, or join the peripatetics, of whom Crothers speaks, and walk back and forth, back and forth in your room, the sermon stuff grows. At last you have before you a pile of half sheets, each with a jotting, a note, an illustration. Out of the chaos order develops, and the dry land of an outline. According to the main heads or headlands of this rough outline, you divide your material into three, four or five piles, or possibly like Robertson into two piles. "Let us see: this thought goes under my II, that under my III, this goes into the Introduction." Then we begin to write, or perhaps we don't.

At this point we divide into two groups. There are men who never write out their sermons in full, there are others who must write every word. I wonder sometimes whether we quite appreciate the possible change that may be wrought in sermon preparation by the invention and prevalent use of the typewriter. There is many a man who in the old days simply did not have the time to write his sermons in full, who finds that his best thoughts come to him as he pounds fast and furiously upon the keys of his typewriter. The mechanical operation of the hands tends to keep the brain and heart active. The homiletical aristocrat may find it possible and wise to dictate to a typist, or preferably to a dictaphone. In three, four hours, the writing is complete. Now he who has written with fury corrects with phlegm. (This is one homiletical instruction that I remember from my seminary days.) There is rearrangement, readjustment. The adjectives are dropped that the gold dust nouns may do the preacher's work for him. The long words are shortened. "When in doubt," says Hare, "use the plainest, the commonest, the most idiomatic. Eschew fine words as you would rouge. Love simple ones as you would native roses on your cheek." We remember the word of Beecher, "Don't whip with a

switch that has the leaves on, if you want to
tingle." Have we fallen unconsciously into
the essay style? We break it up. Here dia-
logue, there question. Have we forgotten
the radical distinction between the teacher's
desk and the preacher's pulpit? We shall
remember now, and reconstruct sentences,
make the past the present, that the ancient
warriors may live again and lead our people
in their long crusade.

Then the preacher draws off a brief preaching outline, which may cover a page or two
of coarsely written catch words. Then the
sermon is laid away until Sunday morning.

Sunday morning comes, always about
forty-eight hours too soon; with it comes an
early breakfast, then two or three hours of
definite pulpit preparation. What shall this
preparation be? There are a few men, I suppose, who must ever be chained to a manuscript. They are fewer than we sometimes
imagine. Our people would usually rather
have us read sermons well prepared than
have us deliver without manuscript sermons
which we should be ashamed to put into
manuscript; but there is no question that
they prefer a good sermon without manuscript to an equally good sermon with manuscript. For most of us the question resolves
itself into this: Are the two or three hours

needful for specific pulpit preparation worth the investment? In ninety cases out of a hundred the time so spent yields dividends of priceless value.

The pulpit preparation is made, not from the manuscript, but from the preaching outline. There is no conscious memorization of the manuscript material, though naturally phrases, sometimes sentences and even whole paragraphs may be uttered as previously written. But that morning in his study the preacher sees them all. There is the young girl, with eager questioning eyes, there the young man who is fighting the half lost fight of virtue, there the grocer whose competitor across the street is underselling him and lying about him. There is the boarding-house keeper whose boarders suddenly, unreasonably left her last week, leaving her with a house rent of fifty dollars to pay at the first of the month. So the preacher thinks through his message for his people. Then ten minutes' walk in God's out-of-doors, then a few moments when with God the preacher shares the silence of eternity, then to the pulpit.

But right here I am interrupted. A preacher tells me, " Man, I have to teach a men's Bible Class immediately before the morning service." I answer, "I beg your pardon, but you do not." If you teach a class before the morning service, you are selling your preacher's birthright, I will not say for a teacher's mess of pottage, but selling it to your great harm and loss.

Into the pulpit the preacher may or may not carry his preaching notes. To some men such notes bring embarrassment, to some they bring just the needed peace and self-control. We probably shall not refer to them at all in the course of the sermon, but they are there, telling us that no crying baby, no fainting woman, no fire-engine siren, need disturb the flow of sermonic thought.

The hymns were chosen before the Sabbath; they harmonize with the preacher's thought and the temper of the sermon. The Scripture reading leads up to or illustrates the idea to be developed. The prayer was thought out in the week time, for the preacher would feel ashamed to speak to God in words less thoughtful than the words he speaks to men. The choirmaster has been gently but firmly reminded that the sermon is not the servant of the choir music, but that the choir music is the servant of the service. The choir has been courteously informed that the choir gallery is not a whispering gallery.

Then the sermon. The whole power of a

kindled personality is at work, not to recall thoughts, words, phrases, paragraphs, but to get God's message into the hearts and lives of God's people. Most instances of poor delivery seem to be instances of inadequate preparation. "Nothing," says one, "is more certain than that the man who has learned early the right modulation of the voice, and has learned to be content with those simple gestures that are natural and dignified, has mastered what is fundamental in pulpit oratory." Some instances of poor delivery are not due to inadequate preparation but to lack of fire. It has been said of Martin Luther that he never did anything well until he was angry. I know laymen who would gladly insult their preacher, if only he would get really "mad" at something, some one, anything, any one. At any rate in our preaching there will always be the note of urgency, of crisis, if you will. "You can't step twice into the same river." No, and you cannot speak twice to the same audience. Even granted that the people composing the congregation Sunday after Sunday are called by the same names, the experiences of the week have made them different people. "This, this is my last chance to speak to these men and women and boys and girls, God's children."

"But I find myself continually harassed by the fear of men." Do you recall the remark of Campbell Morgan? He said that he never felt any nervousness in the pulpit. His friend Thomas Champness replied, "Neither do I, and the reason is the same both in your case and mine,—we have no reputation to lose." May not some such thought help us? The preacher is but a voice. Horton quotes what he calls the grand but singular petition of the Moravian liturgy: "From the unhappy desire of becoming great, Good Lord, deliver me." The herald has no concern for his reputation. He is so identified with his king and his message that he fears the face of no man.

But the most courageous preacher may well fear the face of the clock. The most vicious sermon may have one virtue: it may be brief. How many of us seem to hope by the murder of time to win immortality! I remember one theologue who was gently criticized for preaching for fifty minutes. He replied, "Gunsaulus does." The answer was upon our tongue, but we did not wish to be rude. "A hundred sermons," says Fénelon, "are too long, where one is too short." There are others besides Daniel's Antiochus who wear out the saints of the most high. A half hour to raise the dead? Precisely that; but if a half hour does not suffice to raise the dead, fifty minutes will infallibly seal the tomb.

The preacher had hoped to raise the dead, but after he has pronounced the benediction, and the organ has begun the postlude, as the people stroll out into the light of common day, he can seldom detect a motion of the risen life. Has his word quickened his people? He may hear that one man repeated for himself what R. L. Stevenson once wrote, "I have been to church and am not depressed." Well, that is something. He may chance to hear of a woman who said that after the sermon she felt as did the woman who was accustomed to listen to Beecher: "When I left Plymouth the sun was always shining, whatever the weather." More than this the preacher may never know. But those who have honestly tried to clothe the old message with the new form dictated by their times and their individuality, may be well assured that they have wrought with God in His creative, His recreative, work.

> " And ofttimes cometh our wise Lord God,
>   Master of every trade,
> And tells them tales of daily toil,
>   Of Edens newly made,
> And they rise to their feet as He passes by,
>   Gentlemen unafraid."

III

The Preacher and His Bible

III

THE PREACHER AND HIS BIBLE

THE preacher may be a student of many books. He must be the master of one book, the Bible.

Of this book there is to-day an astounding popular ignorance. Professor Phelps of Yale remarks, "If all the undergraduates of America could be placed in one room, and tested by a common examination on the supposedly familiar stories of the Old Testament, I mean on such instances as Adam, Eve, the Garden of Eden, Noah, Samson, David and Goliath, Moses and Pharaoh, the result would be a magnificent contribution to American humour. The experience of teachers with other books is almost never the same, but ask any teacher in the United States what luck he has with the Bible, and he throws up his hands in despair. I inquired of one fine young specimen of American manhood what he thought Shakespeare meant by the phrase, 'Here feel we not the penalty of Adam,' and he replied, 'It was the mark put on Adam for having slain his brother.' To another lad who was every inch a gentleman, I put the question, 'Explain the line, "Or memorize another Golgotha,"' and his face became a blank. I came to his relief with the remark, 'Golgotha is a New Testament reference.' A light of intelligence illumined his handsome face: 'It was Goliath.'" Professor Phelps declares: "The ignorance of college students of Biblical literature is universal, profound and complete."

I suppose that the Freshmen of a widely known Christian college, which automatically rejects as candidates for the Freshman class the lowest third of the graduating class of any high school, may fairly represent the culture of our intelligent Christian homes. One is continually impressed by the prevailing ignorance. I asked a question regarding the fate of John the Baptist and got this written reply: "Herod, a wicked king disliking John the Baptist, had a large supper and while all were there, John said, 'Whatever ye ask it shall be given you.' And Herod's daughter, following her mother's advice, asked for his head upon a platter. He would not reject her, thus showing his strong faith in God." I do not say that this is typical. I can hardly say it is exceptional.

After numberless experiences of this kind, one trembles to think what would happen should an average Freshman Bible examination be given to an average Sunday congregation. "I will confess," says one of our great English preachers, "that one of the mistakes of my ministry has been my failure to preach with the remembrance of my hearers' disuse of the Scripture." Casual Biblical allusions which we assume to be familiar to our audiences pass them by as doth the idle wind.

Consider the significance of this prevailing ignorance. It means that our people are unfamiliar with the supreme literature of the world. It is a literature supreme in the sublimity of its style. Its style has well been called the style of the heavenly court. Let me read you a few lines:

> "O thou that tellest good tidings to Zion, get
>   thee up on a high mountain;
> O thou that tellest good tidings to Jerusalem,
>   lift up thy voice with strength;
> Lift it up, be not afraid; say unto the cities
>   of Judah, Behold your God."

Think over again the Twenty-third Psalm, "The Lord is my shepherd;" or the first eighteen verses of John, "In the beginning was the Word and the Word was with God and the Word was God." Read again the eighth of Romans, "Who shall separate us from the love of God?" Read again the second of Philippians, "Have this mind in you which was also in Christ Jesus," or the seventh of the Revelation, "These are they that come out of the great tribulation, and they washed their robes, and made them white in the blood of the Lamb. Therefore are they before the throne of God; and they serve him day and night in his temple: and he that sitteth on the throne shall spread his tabernacle over them. They shall hunger no more, neither thirst any more; neither shall the sun strike upon them, nor any heat: for the Lamb that is in the midst of the throne shall be their shepherd, and shall guide them unto fountains of waters of life: and God shall wipe away every tear from their eyes." I do not read language like that anywhere outside the covers of this book.

Again, it is a literature supreme in the variety and the unity of its contents. Here are sixty-six books: history, prophecy, legend, parable, allegory, philosophy, proverbs, familiar correspondence, masterpieces of public discourse, homilies; books written at various times in a period measured by centuries, gathered together and called The Book. The Book was not made one by the fiat of councils. For all its variety the Book is organically one, one with the unity of a common purpose, the unity of a common Presence.

The Bible is a literature supreme in the universality of its appeal. Take a single story, that of the Prodigal Son. Read that story to an audience in a street mission in Singapore or Hong Kong. The hard-faced, soft-hearted sailor, the almond-eyed merchant, the woman whom the world has abandoned, the waif of the street, the student who has come from the West to learn the lore of the East,—there is not one of them whom that single story does not find at the deepest depths of his being.

Again the Bible is a literature supreme in its power. It is the most powerful book in the world. A single verse of the Old Testament, the first, led a young Japanese student, Neesima, to the one God, towards the foundation of the Christian University of the Doshisha. Of a single book of the Old Testament we read, "The psalms have written a new history for themselves in the experience of many Christian men and women, and in some of the memorable movements of the Church and of the world. What a wonderful story they could tell if we could gather it all from lonely chambers, from suffering sickbeds, from the brink of the valley of the shadow of death, from scaffolds and from fiery piles!"

To speak of the Old Testament as a whole:

this was the Bible of John the Baptist. From his favourite prophecy he took the words which expressed his great commission. The Old Testament was the Bible of Jesus. Here the Master found His answers to the Tempter and the warrant for His work of mercy. From the Old Testament, indeed, from one of the prophecies now most completely forgotten, Peter wrought his apologetic at Pentecost. Paul regarded the same Old Testament as the oracles of God. The dry system of laws of which we think almost with aversion, he counted a slave to lead men to the school of Christ. It was the Old Testament which taught the world that "righteousness is salvation."

Turn for a moment from the Old Testament to the New. One verse of that little book caught the eye of a young debauchee named Augustine, and transformed him into a preacher who became at once the father of Romanism and of Protestantism. One verse of that New Testament shook from the soul of Luther the shackles of Romanism, sent him forth, a free man, to set free the western world. Take from the New Testament a single story, that of Jesus, and you take from men the knowledge of Him who hath brought life and immortality out into the light.

It is needless to speak of the New Testa-

ment as a whole.   William Wilberforce tells
us that once on a long journey he read
through the New Testament, and from the
perusal arose, a new creature.   A Hindu well
said, " If I were a missionary, I would not
argue, I would simply say, ' Here is the New
Testament, read that.' "

If we think for a moment of the entire
Bible we remind ourselves that it has puri-
fied languages, it has created literatures.
"The German language," says one, "is
moulded by the Bible."   The Bible has been
the poor man's friend, the handbook of democ-
racy.   We can scarcely quote too often the
words of Green : " No greater moral change
ever passed over a nation than passed over
England during the years which parted the
middle of the reign of Elizabeth from the
meeting of the Long Parliament.   England
became the people of a book, and that book
was the Bible. . . .   Everywhere its words
kindled a startling enthusiasm. . . .   Sunday after Sunday, day after day, the crowds
that gathered round Bonner's Bibles in the
nave of St. Paul's, or the family group that
hung on the words of the Geneva Bible in
the devotional exercises at home were leav-
ened with a new literature. . . .   Elizabeth might silence or tune the pulpits ; but
it was impossible for her to silence or tune

the great preachers of justice, and mercy and truth who spoke from the book she had again opened for her people. . . . A new conception of life and man superseded the old. A new moral and religious impulse spread through every class. . . . The whole nation became, in fact, a Church." The Anglo-Saxon lawmakers have all gone to school to the Bible. The heretics of yesterday, Waldo, Wycliffe, Huss, gained their messages from the Book. The Pilgrims and the Puritans came across the sea to build a new world upon the old Book. It is a true word: "The Hebrews did not make a civilization, but they made a book which has sent other nations to making civilizations." I have read somewhere that the Bible created the idea of humanity. It is certain that the great workers for humanity have been men of the Book. In Africa, the Bible was Livingstone's one trusted guide. Paton, Morrison, Spurgeon, Brooks, Drummond, men of widely differing points of view, were all men of the Book. Of Lincoln it has been said, "He built up his entire reading on his early study of the Bible; he had mastered it absolutely, mastered it as later he mastered very few books." An oriental book, it has worked its way into western life. Become a western book, it now goes back to the East to win dominion. Wherever the Book goes, it makes liars honest, libertines pure, cowards brave. Professor Huxley has remarked, "I have been seriously perplexed to know how the religious feeling which is the essential basis of conduct can be kept up without the use of the Bible."

The Emperor Diocletian made a determined effort to destroy all the copies of the Scripture in his realm. As one thinks of the influence of the Bible upon the history of the world, one is appalled at the thought of what would have happened had he succeeded. And yet Spurgeon's words have sting in them, "The Bible is in every house, but in many the dust on it is so thick that we might write on it: Damnation." If dust gathers upon the Bibles which lie in such saintly but deathlike repose on the lower shelves of the centre tables of our people, Diocletian will achieve his desire without the shedding of blood, always a disagreeable necessity.

Along with the amazing ignorance of the Bible which still prevails, there has developed within the past few years an amazing interest in the Bible. A report compiled December 7, 1913, states that during the preceding year, there had been printed 28,000,000 copies of the Scripture and of portions of the

Scripture. About half of these copies were
in English, the remainder in five hundred
languages and dialects of the world. Add
to this the number of commentaries upon the
Scriptures, the number of Sabbath School
and other printed discussions of the Scriptures, and the quantity of literature is simply
enormous. The life of the average book is
not more than two or four years ; then it is
dead "beyond all hope of resurrection."
Much of the material of the Bible was written
more than twenty-five hundred years ago.
All of it was written more than eighteen hundred years ago. To-day it is the best selling
book in the world. I do not overestimate
the value of such statistics. I recall Mr.
Dooley's discussion of the problem : " Says
I, ' Th' only books in me libr'y is the Bible
an' Shakespeare,' says I. ' They're gr-reat
f'r ye,' says she ; ' so bully f'r th' style.
D'ye read thim all th' time?' she says. ' I
niver read thim,' says I ; ' I use thim f'r purposes iv definse. I have niver read them,
but I'll niver read annything else till I have
read thim,' I says. ' They shtand between
me an' all modhren lithrachoor,' says I.
' I've built thim up into a kind iv break-
wather,' I says, ' an' I set behind it calm and
contint, while Hall Caine rages without,'
says I." But grant the peril, the statistics

remain significant of an extraordinary interest in the Bible.

One of the striking phenomena of our student world is the increase of voluntary Bible study. Among the students of the colleges of the United States and Canada, approximately one hundred thousand women and fifty thousand men are engaged in voluntary Bible study in groups. The Summer Bible Conferences have multiplied. Under the statesmanlike leadership of the Associations of young men and young women, there have been brought together for intensive Bible study thousands of those who are to be leaders of the leaders of our country.

The organized Bible Class movement has spread like wild-fire. Elaborate courses for normal instruction are now being offered by city Sunday-School Associations. Some of our states are giving high school credit for certain specified Biblical work done in the Sabbath School. The Gary plan with its various modifications is likely to give new impetus to Bible study among our boys and girls. Warren H. Wilson speaks with authority of the Sabbath School, which of course centres its work upon the teaching of the Bible : " If only the teachers and ministers realized the value of the Sunday-school and its acceptance with the people, there would be needed no other machinery for building the country community."

Now there is danger in this very revival of interest in the Bible. An unenlightened interest is not so dangerous as utter ignorance. Paul was able to rejoice if Christ were proclaimed whether in truth or in pretense. But when one remembers that Luther's hostile attitude towards Copernicus was determined by his attitude towards Scripture, when one remembers the witchcraft delusion of Salem, and all the crimes that have been committed in obedience to Scripture, one notes with chilled enthusiasm certain aspects of the revived interest in the Bible. A new interest in the Bible leads one man to become a Mormon, another to become a disciple of Dowie. Bible classes organized under the auspices of certain schools of thought are likely to lead to darkness and to ditches as often as to daylight and the great ascent.

Has not the preacher come to his kingdom for such a time as this? The preacher does not have to fight for his place. He is universally recognized as the authorized interpreter of Scripture. He is supposed to be a Biblical expert. In this field he has no competition to fear. The Bible is the preacher's Book. A spectator sometimes wonders whether we preachers have quite appreciated our strategic position, wonders whether we might not declare a closed season for pulpit discussions of the latest novel. Professor Moulton, a critic of literature, is able to pack a church even on a prayer-meeting night. The people come to hear him read the Bible in a way that gives sense. If we can interpret Browning, Milton, Winston Churchill, Ernest Poole, well and good. But if we use them to draw our audiences and to preach our sermons for us, are we not silently giving notice to the community, "In these days of popular ignorance of the Bible, yet increasing interest in the Bible, in these days of rampant and widely advertised misinterpretations of the Bible, I believe it is impossible to interest this community in the one book concerning which I am supposed to speak with expert knowledge and authority"? Do not the people of the community read that silent notice, when they read our advertisement of what we regard as a more attractive program than that of Biblical preaching?

Why do we not possess our possessions? I believe one reason to be this: All of us as preachers are affected, infected by the American tendency to change. With childlike simplicity we stake our success upon method.

The method fails, it must be wrong ; we must try another method. We tried the Boys' Scouts. They " petered out." We tried the Knights of King Arthur. We gave up that organization. Why? Was there anything wrong about the method? There may have been everything right about the method. No method will work, unless there is a man to work the method. We tried to preach Biblical sermons, but the people were not interested. Was there anything wrong about the method? The prime necessity is not a new method, but a new conscience, a new confidence, a new enthusiasm, a new man. Old things are passed away, behold *they* are become new.

In parenthesis it ought perhaps to be said that there are doubtless circumstances that will beat any man. It is to be questioned whether a man can successfully preach Biblical sermons or any other kind of sermons in a church which ought to be burned to the ground in the interest of the kingdom of God. It ought also to be added that most of us are victims of " the lust for statistics." I would not indeed think that a minister proved his spirituality or preaching power by emptying his church, but are we not all greatly indebted to Dr. Jefferson for insisting on the difference between getting an audience and building a church? I am persuaded that in trying to win an audience a man may undermine his church and lose his preacher's soul.

But I suspect that our failure to possess our possessions is largely due to the influence of modern Biblical scholarship. With cheerful heart and without reservation, we used to quote as equally authoritative verses of Scripture wherever found, in Ecclesiastes or Ephesians, in Esther the book of the bigot or in the Logia of Jesus. We used to treat as of equal historicity the story of Noah's voyage in the ark and the story of Paul's voyage in the ship of Adramyttium. We used to delve into and delight in word studies. Our task was to harmonize passages of Scripture, so as to frame a system of Biblical theology, which we thought was preachable whether it was rational or not. If some passages absolutely refused to submit to our treatment, we allegorized them, and regarded the allegory as a demonstration rather than an illustration.

In our study of prophetism we emphasized prediction as its chief element, failing to realize the truth of the word of J. M. P. Smith: "The prophets insisted constantly that the present was the future in the making, and that there could not possibly be any divorce between the two. Prediction then was to some extent a homiletical method for achieving moral and spiritual results in the present." One needs but to read the libretto of the oratorio of the " Messiah," and then in the light of modern scholarship, to read the texts which Handel used, to perceive what a change has taken place in the preacher's point of view. We had been wont to look out upon the future through the windows of the Apostle Paul, and seldom noticed that the windows of John offered somewhat different vistas, nor did we recognize the fact that the windows of both alike were stained here and there by the radiance of the current apocalyptic.

Biblical scholarship has called to its aid all history, archæology, comparative literature and religion, the psychology of religion, a new world view. Questions have paralyzed our hitherto dogmatic assertions. The censer bearer in Christ's triumph train becomes not seldom the herald, to use Mathews' phrase, " of the good news of pentateuchal analysis " ; the crusader becomes the critic ; and you recall the definition of the critic, " A critic is the valet who brushes the clothes of the truth." I am bound to add with all respect that often the valet bungles his job, and frays or soils the clothes. The man who has supposed himself to be breathing the free airs on the mountain top of truth now breathes and breathes out the airs of a spiritual dissecting-room. I do not say that this is the characteristic influence of the historical criticism. I do say that upon many men it has exerted this influence. But surely, brethren, these things ought not, need not, so to be. Surely we betray a singular lack of faith in God and in His word.

Suppose we think for a moment with a man who has just come under the influence of modern Biblical scholarship, an influence which indeed no man can escape. Let us see what encouragements there are for this man as he faces the facts.

First comes to the preacher's remembrance the glorious ancient word carved on the front wall of the New York Library, "But above all things truth beareth away the victory." Then comes to his remembrance the word of Huxley, "Science seems to me to teach in the highest and strongest manner the great truth which is embodied in the Christian conception of entire surrender to the will of God. Sit down before fact as a little child, be prepared to give up every preconceived notion, follow humbly wherever and to whatever abysses nature leads, or you shall learn nothing." And the preacher determines to sit down before fact, if only he can find it, before fact as a little child.

Then for his sober encouragement in meet-

ing facts comes that word of George Adam
Smith. We are reminded that he looked
through the vast correspondence of Henry
Drummond; that "some letters came from
the silence and loneliness of the far margins
of our world, some came from the centres
of civilization. One and all told how the
literal acceptance of the Bible was what had
driven them away from religion." He writes,
"It is astonishing how many of the questions
had to do with the Old Testament, with its
discrepancies, its rigorous laws, its pitiless
tempers, its open treatment of sexual questions, the atrocities related by history and
sanctioned by law." The preacher recalls
from his own observation more than one
instance of the tragic recoil from literalism
to infidelity. Again the preacher takes heart
of hope as he remembers that while modern
scholarship makes it almost unendurable to
read certain old preachers of the second rank,
the old preachers of the first rank, men who
knew nothing of our higher criticism, speak
to us still with an intense, vital, exigent present day appeal and power. The preacher
then considers the notable fact brought out
by Dr. Bosworth that alone of the religions
of the world, Christianity has dared to subject its sacred books to the most searching
scrutiny. How fine it is to think that we

are not afraid to be investigated. He gathers up the positive results of this criticism. For example, the prophets who were buried in nicely whitewashed tombs come forth to live again, strong men, human men, heroes by the grace of God, men who long to share with us their visions of God and God's will, men who would tell us how to fight our beautiful fight. Think of the fact that in the study of Jonah we find not so much the opportunity to discuss the capacity of a whale's belly, as the opportunity to disclose the gospel before the Gospel, to enter into the prophet's thought of the length and breadth and height and depth of the love of God.

The preacher remembers that this same Biblical scholarship has given back to us the historical Jesus, whom we were in danger of losing. A writer calls our attention to the fact that " every life of Christ worth reading outside the Gospels has been written since 1835, that therefore our generation knows the historical life of Christ more perfectly than any generation since Christ was on earth, can judge more accurately and inter-pret more certainly the meaning of His every act and word." Our study of the mystery cults helps us see that Paul used terms which his age could understand in order to state what to him was the worth of Christ. Our study of the Logos doctrine helps us see how the writer of the fourth Gospel strove to carry over the good news of Jesus into the atmosphere of Greek culture, and sought to state in terms of the generation which he knew, the value of the Jesus whom he knew and loved. The preacher is now able to gather up every bit of broken light which has shone from God upon his brother man anywhere, and is able in turn to share with him the white light of the knowledge of the glory of God in the face of Jesus Christ. Our Biblical scholarship has set us free from what has been called adjectival Christianity, and has saved to us a substantive Christianity which can be preached, and a Bible which needs no league of defense.

We have often been told that to a great life two factors are essential, work and friendship. The real secret of the power of the Bible has been this, that it has introduced men to the supreme work and to the supreme friendships of the world. Biblical scholarship has not lost to the Bible its secret. On the contrary, at this moment, the Bible reveals to us in new and beautiful fashion the great work and the great friendships.

Modern scholarship has brought into more

vivid light the age-long power of the Bible
to introduce men to the kind of work which
alone can permanently satisfy men.   To-day
it calls to men, " Work for the kingdom of
God : work for the world-wide society of the
brotherly sons of God.   That work will bind
all the tasks of life into one lifelong task.
That work will call out your highest enthusiasm from sunrise to sunset."   When a man
catches a vision of the task to which the Bible
and the Bible alone of books introduces him,
all tasks seem cheap and tawdry, unless they
can be subordinated to, made a part of the
eternal and eternally satisfying task.

Modern scholarship, as we have said, has
only made more obvious the persistent power
of the Bible to introduce men to the great
friendships of the great life.   The Bible to-
day welcomes men to the vital friendship of
Amos, the dresser of sycomore-trees, who
entered as it were the Westminster Abbey
of Israel, to deliver his message of God's
law ; to the friendship of Hosea, who crossed
the threshold of his ruined home, to speak
to men of the sin which breaks the heart as
well as the law of God.   Alone of books, the
Bible is able to acquaint men with Elijah,
the man who stood before Jehovah, with
Jeremiah, the man who looked up from the
pit and saw the stars ; with Peter, the pas-

sionate, disloyal, loyal friend of Jesus ; with the disciple whom Jesus loved, the man who leaned upon the Master's breast at supper and stood by the Master at the cross. Alone of the books of the world, the Bible is able to introduce men to a vital friendship with God, and this primarily because the Bible alone is able to introduce men to Jesus, the revealer of the Father. This is the persistent wonder of the Book, that it can guide the beggar, the peasant, the prince, into the court of heaven, there to sit beside the King upon His throne.

The sovereign power of the Book is not a memory. Nor will that power pass with the process of the suns. No new researches of comparative religion, no new discoveries or pseudo-discoveries of archæologists, no newspaper announcements that Noah rather than Eve ate the fatal apple, can hurt the preacher. All truth is his. Scholarship serves, but no longer scares him. The Lord Jehovah hath given him the tongue of them that are taught that he may know how to sustain with words him that is weary. He wakeneth morning by morning, He wakeneth his ear to hear as they that are taught. And the Lord Jehovah wakens His disciple's ear most often and most surely with the sustaining and sympathetic words of the Word of God.

The preacher who has come inevitably under the influence of modern Biblical scholarship needs simply to remember Campbell Morgan's story : George Borrow when taken by a guide to see the sources of the Severn and the Wye, insisted, not only on seeing, but on drinking the pure spring waters. "I must drink deeply of these springs," he said, "that I may speak of them with authority."

What then? At all hazards let us give to our people the Bible. No Sunday service need be an absolute failure if the preacher will read with understanding and power the great utterances of Scripture. If the evening audience is small, the preacher may decide to remove the pulpit from the platform, transform his congregation into a Bible class, with its blackboard, its mimeographed outlines, its Socratic method. With deliberation the preacher may become the teacher. It is barely possible that a man may decide to combine into one service of instruction and inspiration the Bible School and the preaching service of the morning. But rather than employ these somewhat dubious experiments let us be ambitious to be Biblical preachers. Let us heed the implied exhortation of the words spoken of Frederick W. Robertson, "Perhaps the first thing that arrests our attention is the distinctively

Biblical quality of his preaching. He illustrates most suggestively the fruitfulness of Biblical study for homiletic use, furnishes the most attractive model of effective Biblical method, and has exerted an important influence upon the best Biblical preaching of our day."

Let us treat our texts with honest reverence. Let us not hurry away from them, as Cook's tourists from the supreme treasures of European art galleries, as all of us from the infinitely precious commonplaces of life. How significant are the words of Ruskin's friend, who had been asked to make a visit to Rome : "I ought to go with you to Rome, but my difficulty is to appreciate my own back garden, our copper beech, our weeping ash, our little nailed up rose tree, and twisting nailed up creepers. I think when I have finished with the back garden, I will go as far as Rome."

We shall preach more expository sermons. Beecher and Brooks both advocate this by precept if not by example. Jowett urges it by example if not by precept. In introducing one sermon he says, "If I were to repeat my text this morning, I should have to repeat the whole of the Epistle to the Colossians. I think it is well that at times we should get away from inspecting the individual flower however beautiful, and even away from the wonders of the single hedgerow, and the glories of the larger garden or field, and ascending some conspicuous height contemplate and comprehend some commanding landscape. And I think it is well even in public worship that we should occasionally get away from the winsomeness of some particular text, and climbing some available height, survey a wide expanse of Christian truth such as is unveiled to us in one of the letters of the Apostle Paul, and I do not think that exercise was ever more necessary than it is to-day."

By the expository sermon we may do two things : We may enforce the lesson we wish to teach, and at the same time do what we seldom do in a topical sermon, we may help our people to fall in love with the Bible itself. In the passage we propose to expound, we shall seek one mother idea within whose ample embrace all the children ideas may be gathered, not to fight but to help each other. We shall heed Horton's advice, and never stay more than twelve months away from any portion of the Scripture. With our people we shall think of the morning stories of Genesis, show their points of similarity to the stories of the Babylonish world, yet their wonderful superiority. We shall take the story of the fall, note the fidelity of the old legend to the permanent facts of life ; for example, the temptation which so subtly appeals to the entirely legitimate and laudable aspiration for self-realization, the sin which seeks comradeship, but which casts the blame upon the fellow sinner and finally back upon God Himself,—" The woman whom *thou* didst give me,"—the sin which begets fear and guilt and brings a curse upon all nature and all life. Occasionally we shall turn to Scriptural legislation. We shall bid our people construct battlements for the roof, that the place of rest and of play and of prayer may be made safe. In a brief, perhaps casual way we shall compare and contrast the Mosaic Code with the Code of Hammurabi. We shall glory in the fact that God hath spoken unto the legislators not alone of one nation. Every law whether in or out of the Bible, we shall bring into the presence of Jesus, by Him to be judged. If our people are inclined to emphasize externals, we may lead them by the way of the ancient covenant past Jeremiah's dream of a new covenant, up to Jesus' ratification of the new covenant at the Last Supper, on into the life of the new covenant as Paul reveals it in II Corinthians.

We shall spend much time with the New

Testament correspondence, then swing back
into the hymn-book of the second temple, to
hear once more the silver trumpets calling us
to worship, to see once more the pilgrims in
whose hearts are the highways to Zion.   For
a while we shall sit down with Job, as he
studies with eyes washed clean by tears the
problem of his pain.   We shall listen to
Koheleth as he concludes that that which is
crooked can never become straight, that there
is nothing better for a man than that he
should eat and drink and make his soul
enjoy good in his labour.   We shall then
listen to the prophet as he hurls back the
triumphant word, " The crooked shall become
straight," or to Paul as he cries, " I am persuaded that neither death nor life, nor angels
nor principalities, nor things present nor
things to come, nor powers, nor height nor
depth, nor any other creature shall be able to
separate us from the love of God, which is in
Christ Jesus our Lord."

We shall spend much time in the study of
the biographies of the obscure pilgrims of the
Road.   Here is Andrew, the quiet man who
was always introducing men to Jesus.   Here is
Onesiphorus, the man whose heathen parents
had named him at birth, " Profit-bearer," but
who later became a Christian.   No profit-
bearer now !   But he happened to be in

Rome, remembered that there was a certain near-sighted Jew by the name of Paul who was spending the last months of his life in some jail. From prison to prison he went, inquired for Paul, found him, came again and yet again to see him, refreshed him, cooled him off, as Paul puts it. His coming was like a breath from the Alban hills to the aged prisoner of Jesus. But surely the man was untrue to his name? Not so. He brought profit to the apostle, and to Timothy, yes, and to his household. What would you like to leave to your children at your death? A few dollars which your sons may use or lose? Would you not rather have the prayers of some apostle of Jesus Christ, calling down upon them God's blessings from the heights of heaven? But surely Onesiphorus was unprofitable to himself? A man mustn't melt himself down into oil for the tallow trade. Well, how much would you give for a half hour's talk with the Apostle Paul? Would you insist on damask cushions? Would you insist on an airy front office overlooking the harbour, a room with electric lights and a buzzing electric fan?

Most often shall we bid our people look upon Jesus as He walks through the gardens and along the roads of Galilee and of our own dear land.

"Behold him now where He comes !
  Not the Christ of our subtle creeds,
  But the Lord of our hearts, of our homes,
  Of our hopes, our prayers, our needs ;
  The brother of want and blame,
  The lover of women and men,
  With a love that puts to shame
  All passions of mortal ken."

Have you never had this experience ? You have been preaching away to a soggy, sodden, sleepy congregation, and then you spoke of Jesus, and each man awoke as if he caught "sight of a sweepy garment vast and white, with a hem that he could recognize."

An old professor of mine remarks, " Some preachers are always on castors." I believe one reason for their extraordinary mobility is their failure as Biblical preachers. The minister must run away before his material runs out. The words of William Watson, written indeed with another thought in mind, are specially pertinent to the preacher and his use of the Bible.

" The knights rode up with gifts for the king,
  And one was a jewelled sword,
  And one was a suit of golden mail,
  And one was a golden Word.

" He buckled the shining armour on
  And he girt the sword at his side ;
  But he flung at his feet the golden Word
  And trampled it in his pride.

> "The armour is pierced with many spears,
> And the sword is breaking in twain;
> But the Word hath risen in storm and fire
> To vanquish and to reign."

The preacher who makes his own *the* golden Word, with that golden Word shall rise to reign in the kingdom of the preacher.

"You have apparently implied that, as we have been inevitably influenced by the historical criticism, we are bound to preach it. Do you believe this?" That was a fine prayer of an old Union Seminary friend of mine, "From half baked Drivers, Cheynes and Briggses in the pulpit, Good Lord, deliver us." In the frank and intimate fellowship, give and take, question and answer of the Normal Bible Class we shall lead our people into the liberating truths of the modern scholarship. In the pulpit we shall assume and use the assured results of historical criticism, but shall not label them. In general we shall burn our own smoke. I came upon this fascinating translation of Paul's advice to his callow theologue friend, Timothy: "Adjure them before the Lord not to bandy arguments—no good comes out of that, it only means the undoing of your audience. Do your utmost to let God see that you at least are a sound workman, with no need to be ashamed of the way you handle the word of the Truth.   Shut your mind against foolish, popular controversy; be sure that only breeds strife.   And the Lord's servant must not be a man of strife; he must be kind to everybody, a skilled teacher, a man who will not resent injuries; he must be gentle in his admonitions to the opposition—God may perhaps let them change their mind and admit the Truth; they may come to their senses again and escape the snare of the devil, as they are brought back to life by God to do His will."

Of course the preacher has no right to make his pulpit "a coward's castle," and no man enters the kingdom of the preacher without tribulation.   But I ask you to notice that there are two kinds of men who in days past have died violent deaths.   There are the men whom the world crowns as martyrs, God's witnesses. There are the men whom the world compassionates or condemns as fanatics and fools.   The minister who says : "I am going to tell the truth, the whole truth and nothing but the truth, always and under all circumstances and to all men," deserves the fate he invites, and does not need to pose for a moment as a martyr.   When a man writes me that he has been driven from his church for preaching the higher criticism, I am inclined to send him back this syllogism and ask him to discover the fallacy :

All prophets suffer.
You suffer.
Therefore you are a prophet.

George A. Gordon remarks that the best thing he got out of his seminary days was the word of a Methodist minister : " God and a fool might do as much good in the world as God and a wise man, but they have never done it."

Paul was no coward, but when he was dealing with babies, he gave them milk. To the last Jesus withheld some truths from His disciples, because they could not bear them. No preacher will go far wrong in his use of the Bible if he is able reverently to make his own the words of Jesus, " The spirit of the Lord is upon ME because the Lord hath anointed ME to preach good tidings to the poor, to proclaim release to the captives, and recovering of sight to the blind, to set at liberty them that are bruised, to proclaim the acceptable year of the Lord."

Let us teach our people first to trust our love, our faith, our honesty AND our wisdom. If our people trust our love, our faith, our honesty AND our wisdom, then they will follow us, though at times we lead them by new paths to " the fair world, and the beautiful lights of heaven,"

IV

Abraham Lincoln: The Preacher's Teacher

IV

ABRAHAM LINCOLN: THE PREACH-
ER'S TEACHER

NOT all of us are called preachers, but all of us are interested or wish we were interested in preaching. A friend said to me, "I am perfectly willing to serve the church. I should be entirely willing to shovel coal into the furnace but I do not like to listen to sermons;" and yet this very man would have listened with rapt attention to Phillips Brooks. And I suspect that most of us would subscribe to the words of the writer who says: "The churches are made up of plain people, and the plain people always know what they want. Faddists may think that the day of preaching has gone by, but the churches have never been so certain as they are to-day that the man most essential in extending the work of the kingdom of God is the preacher."

What is more, all of us are in a very real sense preachers bearing by the lips some sort of life message. Particularly true is this of Congregationalists, for I never heard of a Congregationalist who belonged to the submerged and silent multitude. I would speak then of Lincoln as our teacher in the fine art of preaching.

February is a month of memories. We remember the birthday of Washington; we remember the birthday of Lincoln. There are other memories. On February 4, 1861, the delegates from six seceding states met at Montgomery, Alabama. On February 9, 1861, Jefferson Davis was elected President of the Confederacy. On February 11, 1861, Lincoln left Springfield for Washington, borrowing money enough we are told to pay the expenses of his first few months in the White House. A few days later he eluded the first attempt at assassination. On February 23, he reached the capital.

Glance for a moment at the task which faced our teacher on that February day of 1861. It was a twofold task. Lincoln understood at the time but half of it. The first half of his task was the preservation of the Union; and yet we read, " Before his inauguration the seceding states had control of practically every fort, arsenal, dockyard, mint, customs-house, court-house in their entire territory." Robert E. Lee, whom Scott regarded as the ablest officer in the army, resigned and took command of the forces of Virginia. A federal army of less than

20,000 men, and these widely scattered, was at Lincoln's command. The sentiment at the North was divided. Many blatant politicians insisted that Lincoln should belie the promises of his platform and compromise with the South for the sake of unity. Many of the most influential orators and newspapers insisted that we should allow " our erring Southern sisters to depart in peace."

The second half of Lincoln's task as it developed was the abolition of slavery. And yet as Lincoln said in his second inaugural address, " One-eighth of the whole population were coloured slaves, not widely distributed over the union, but localized in the southern part of it. These slaves constituted a peculiar and powerful interest." Slavery had affected the whole life of the nation. Scarcely a vote was cast at the polls, scarcely a decision was rendered in a court of justice, scarcely a dollar's worth of business was transacted, but upon it fell the shadow of the curse. Meanwhile in 1861, the thought of immediate abolition was the thought of a few so-called "sciolists" and fanatics. Truly "the pilot was hurried to the helm in a tornado."

What of the pilot? A child of poverty, his father barely able to scrawl his name, his mother buried one dismal day, her coffin made of green lumber, cut by the father's whip-saw; a lad with about a year's schooling all told; a young man with his dreams, his loves, his disappointments, his great sorrows; a rural lawyer, a legislator of the frontier, a congressman of one term, and now a man fifty-two years of age, an old man, as he calls himself, a poor man. In a letter dated 1860, he writes, " I could not raise ten thousand dollars if it would save me from the fate of John Brown."

The task then, a task which Lincoln said was greater than that which rested upon Washington, and the man? Can we wonder that the people of the East looked cold and sad? And yet the man, this man, met and mastered his task,

> " Grew up a destined work to do
> And lived to do it—four long-suffering years;
> Ill-fate, ill-feeling, ill-report, lived through,
> And then he heard the hisses change to cheers."

The Union was saved, slavery was abolished. "He bound the Union, he unbound the slave." This man finished his "great job." A contemporary cartoon represents Lincoln holding in his hand an envelope inscribed "Thirteenth Amendment to the Constitution." He smiles and says, "This is like a dream I once had in Illinois." The dream of Lincoln's life had come true.

Before us, preachers all, lies not indeed
the same task as that of Lincoln. We do not
unduly magnify our office if we compare our
task with his. Each minister of the Gospel in
pulpit or in pew is a leader of those forces
which are seeking to bind the union, not of
states, but of men, not in the bonds of political unity, but in the bonds of "a world-wide
civilization of friendly workmen." Each
preacher is a leader of those forces which are
seeking to unbind the slaves of evil conditions and of evil dispositions, to lift the arti-
ficial burdens from the shoulders and the
hearts of men, to give to all men "a fair chance
at all good things." And here are we, men
who feel profoundly inadequate to our task,
like Lincoln, it may be, with little education,
with little prestige among the élite, with
empty purse. " But," you say, "the analogy
does not hold good, for Lincoln controlled the
armies and the navies and the boundless resources of the nation, and he dedicated them
all to the relentless crushing of the foe."
That's true ; but mark you, he could not have
compelled army, navy or resources for twenty-
four months except by the methods which are
at our command, the methods of persuasion,
the methods of the preacher.

And perhaps the first suggestion that our
teacher would make to us is this, that the

preacher does not need to be prepossessing. You recall the man who solemnly gave Lincoln a jack-knife, saying, " This knife was placed in my hands some years ago with the injunction that I was to keep it until I should find a man uglier than I was. Allow me to say, sir, that I think you are fairly entitled to this property " Closing an autobiographical sketch written in 1859, Lincoln says, " If any personal description of me is thought desirable, it may be said I am in height six feet, four inches nearly, lean in flesh, weighing on an average one hundred and eighty pounds, dark complexion, with coarse black hair and gray eyes. No other marks or brands recollected." Men were quick to note

> " His length of shambling limb, his furrowed face,
>   His gaunt, gnarled hands, his unkempt, bristling
>   hair,
>   His garb uncouth, his bearing ill at ease,
>   His lack of all we prize as debonair,
>   Of power or will to shine, of art to please."

And yet we are told that when he was awakened he became transfigured, so that a man who heard him said, " He was the handsomest man I ever saw." And our teacher raises this query : If, homely as we are, we could just once, only once be thoroughly awakened, would not our very homeliness become handsome ?

Lincoln hasn't much to teach us regarding delivery. His gestures were sometimes strangely awkward. In his debates with Douglass, he had a way, we are told, of coming down, bending his knees, and then rising up to more than his full height. This habit gradually wore away ; but one would not study his gestures to imitate them. Nor need we envy the voice of our teacher. It is said that he had a high pitched tenor voice, rising at times of emotion into a falsetto ; but there is one thing to be noted : " His voice could carry farther than Douglass's heavy basso." Nor did he trust implicitly the range of his voice. When he was about to give his famous Cooper Union speech, he planned that a friend should sit in the rear of the room and lift his umbrella if the speaker could not be easily heard. Perhaps none of us has a vice more irritating than that of dropping the voice at the end of each sentence, so that if the congregation follows the discourse at all, it is by skill in lip-reading.

Has Lincoln anything to teach us as to the choice of words ? The words of his choice were not merely the happy inspiration of the untrained linguist. When preparing his telegrams for the front, we read, he would sit a long while chewing the end of his pen, a habit of his, until he found the right word.

Seldom is this right word one of the great mouth-filling words. Almost always it is a word chosen from the common speech of common men.

In a certain town, not two thousand miles away from Oberlin, a little girl sat in church with her mother, and whispered, "Mama, what is the minister trying to say?" "Why, my dear, he is telling us to be good." "Oh, I wish he would stop, I will be good. I want to hear the music again." How many of our hearers would agree at once to be good, if we would only stop, or else use the language of the homes and the hearts of men.

> " Think not that strength lies in the big round word,
>   Or that the brief and plain must needs be weak.
>   There is a strength
>   Which dies if stretched too far or spun too fine,
>   Which has more height than breadth, more depth
>   than length.
>   Let but this force of thought and speech be mine,
>   And he that will may take the sleek fat phrase,
>   Which glows and burns not, though it gleam and
>   shine,
>   Light but not heat, a flash but not a blaze."

There is a story told of a literary genius, who at night would wake stung by the splendour of a sudden thought, and would say to his wife, "Mary, get up and light a candle; I have thought of a good word." At last the

worm turned: "William," said Mary one
night, "get up yourself and light a candle;
I have thought of a bad word." And yet
with some risk to family felicity, we might
still be blest, should we take more care to
choose the good word, always remembering
that particularly good word of Lowell, "The
highest outcome of culture is simplicity."

Let us question our teacher somewhat
further, and ask him of his style of speech.
I suspect that he thought comparatively little
about it, and yet he was not indifferent to it,
and we know that an eminent teacher of
English at Yale followed him about in New
England, that he might learn and teach the
secret of his strength.

You are all familiar with the sermon of
Dr. Hitchcock, entitled, "The Eternal Atone-
ment." Professor Bliss of Palestine Explora-
tion fame told me that he read this sermon
once a twelvemonth for the tonic of thought:
but mark the language here and there. For
example: "The Hebrew mind as represented
by Philo was only just beginning to be trini-
tarian when Christ's life in the flesh compelled
the Hebrew mind as represented by Peter and
Paul and John to a new theology. After
Pentecost, bald unitarianism was anach-
ronous. Christian experience logically required three divine persons, of one and the

same divine essence. Economic trinity required essential trinity." Now I know that to you this is clear as "a cloudless moon." But theologues who have read this sermon as a task of the curriculum have expressed the wish that Hitchcock had studied at the feet of Lincoln.

As we study Lincoln's style, we note its exceeding compression. Perhaps you should expect this compression in telegrams; but take this sent to McClellan, " I have just received your despatch about sore-tongued and fatigued horses. Will you pardon me for asking what the horses of your army have done since the battle of Antietam that fatigues anything?" Or this to Grant: "General Sheridan says, 'If the thing is pressed, I think that Lee will surrender.' Let the thing be pressed." One might perhaps expect this compression of style in a casual note of commendation like this: "My dear sir, the lady, bearer of this, says she has two sons who want to work. Wanting to work is so rare a want that it should be encouraged." But take this typical remark: " Grant is a copious worker and fighter, but a very meager writer or telegrapher."

In a letter to James Conkling, there is a striking illustration of this compression of style. " There are those who are dissatisfied

with me. To such I would say, You desire
peace, and you blame me that you do not
have it. But how can we attain it? There
are but three conceivable ways; first to suppress the rebellion by force of arms; this I
am trying to do. Are you for it? If you
are, so far we are agreed. If you are not
for that, a second way is to give up the
Union. I am against this. Are you for it?
If you are, you should say so plainly. If
you are not for force, nor yet for dissolution,
there only remains some imaginable compromise. I do not believe that any compromise
embracing the maintenance of the Union is
now possible." Carl Schurz explains this
characteristic of style: " As a boy, Abe soon
felt the impulse to write, not only making
extracts from books which he wished to remember, but also composing little essays of
his own. First he sketched these with char-
coal on a wooden shovel, scraped white with
a drawing knife, or on bass-wood shingles,
then he transferred them to paper, which was
a scarce commodity in the Lincoln household, taking care to cut his expressions close
so that they might not cover too much space."
With us paper is too cheap. A while ago a
friend of mine was asked to write a daily
hundred word sermon for the newspaper. It
was a " salt and bitter and good " experience.

Again our teacher would bid us speak in such fashion as to compel our hearers' ears to serve as eyes. In the art he urges, Lincoln is himself past master. Note his method. "Every man, black, white or yellow, has a mouth to be fed, and two hands with which to feed it, and bread should be allowed to go to that mouth without controversy." And at once you see three men, one black, one white, one yellow, the mouth of each man, the two hands of each reaching for the bread to convey it to the mouth. Again: "Douglass thinks he sees the last tip of the last joint of the old serpent's tail just drawing out of sight;" or again: "The Judge thinks that the Almighty has drawn a moral climate line across the continent, on one side of which labour must be performed by slaves." Knowing well the value of visualization, he urges us by his practice to use germ parables. "You will not abide the election of a Republican president. In that supposed event, you say, we will destroy the Union. And then you say the great crime of having destroyed it will be upon us. That is cool. A highwayman holds a pistol to my ear, and mutters through his teeth, 'Stand and deliver, or I shall kill you, and then you will be a murderer.'" Or again, "I do not allow myself to suppose that either the convention or the

League have concluded that I am either the greatest or the best man in America, but rather they have concluded that it is not best to swap horses while crossing the river, and have further concluded that I am not so poor a horse that they might not make a botch of it in trying to swap."

Every now and then the germ, we observe, should be developed into a full blown parable. Permit me to remind you of two familiar and famous illustrations. He is speaking of the proposed expansion of slavery into the territories. "If I find a venomous snake lying on the open prairie I seize the first stick and kill him at once, but if the snake is in bed with my children, I must be more cautious lest I shall, in striking the snake, also strike the children or rouse the reptile to bite the children. But if the question is whether to kill it on the prairie or put it in bed with the other children, I am inclined to think we'd kill it." The illustration has all the force of a demonstration.

His critics came to him quite distracted by his sins of omission and commission. "Gentlemen, suppose that all the property you were worth was in gold, and you had put it in the hands of Blondin to carry across the Niagara River on a rope, would you shake the cable, or keep shouting to him,

' Blondin, stand up a little straighter; Blondin, stoop a little more, go a little faster, lean a little more to the north, lean a little more to the south '?   No, you would hold your breath as well as your tongue and keep your hands off until he was safe over." That parable needs no elucidation.

Our people are surrounded by innumerable appeals to the eye. There has been a great change in this matter even since some of us younger men began to preach. No magazine except the *Hibbert Journal* and the *Atlantic* without its pictures, no newspaper without its cuts and cartoons. The theatres and moving picture shows all speak to the eye. Charles M. Sheldon has learned to speak to the eye. At the other pole of platform speech is Billy Sunday. Can we doubt for a moment that much of his unquestioned power arises from his ability to make men see with their eyes the things which they hear with their ears?

I jot down in my note-book another suggestion of our teacher, namely, that a deadly earnestness of speech is entirely compatible with the play of humour. Lincoln's humour is not always very subtle. In his early days he sees Adam and Eve at work, "sewing aprons, the first sewing society, the mother of all sewing societies." Later he tells us that Douglass's popular sovereignty idea "is being simmered down until it has become as thin as the homœopathic soup made by boiling the shadow of a pigeon that has starved to death." But he is always being reminded of a story. When friends come to him to tell him of a beautiful way to end the war, he is reminded of a man who was trying to head up a barrel, but found that the boards always fell in. A brilliant idea came to him. He would put his little boy inside to hold up the boards. The plan succeeded to admiration, but the man found to his surprise and regret that he had nailed his little boy inside. When some citizens propose a naval diversion in the South, he is reminded of an old lady of Salem, who had a singing in her head, and put a plaster of psalm tunes on her feet to draw the singing down.

I know it is easy to win the reputation of the buffoon, the court fool. There is no sadder death to die than the death of the after-dinner speaker; but by his humour Lincoln drew the poison from the fangs of madness, and kept his own mind sane. Can you not see the Master smile as he tells of the devil who goes out of a man, wanders about in waterless places, seeking rest and finding none; who thinks of the old homestead, discovers it empty, swept and garnished, and brings trooping after him seven other devils worse than himself? The laughter which laughs never at people, but with people, helps to carry a strong man's message to men.

And in this speech of Lincoln's, so compressed, so concrete and picturesque, so shot through with humour, there is always an extraordinary directness of address. " Let me talk to some gentleman down there who looks me in the face," this at Quincy ; or again at Alton, " Let me take the gentleman who looks me in the face and let us suppose that he is a member of the territorial legislature." Always he seems to be saying to each of his hearers : " I am not talking to the crowd of people down there : I want to take YOU by the hand and reason this thing out with you personally, sure that we shall agree just as soon as we understand the matter aright." " Watch me as I sail up into the empyrean ! " None of that. " Come now and let us reason together." So shall a man become a persuader of men.

I may have given the impression that in this speech of his there is little of dignity, beauty, distinction ; but we should wrong our teacher by leaving such an impression. It is true that in the early days there was a

good deal of that flamboyant speech which
still characterizes some of our sophomoric
contests. For example, in 1842, as he speaks
on temperance he says, "Happy day, when
all appetites controlled, all poisons subdued,
all matter subjected, mind, all conquering
mind, shall live and move the monarch of the
world. Glorious consummation. Hail, fall
of Fury, Reign of Reason, all hail." Of
course this is pretty bad; but mark the
change and listen to his words uttered little
more than a month before his death: "Fondly
do we hope, fervently do we pray that this
mighty scourge of war may speedily pass
away. Yet if God wills that it continue until
all the wealth piled by the bondman's two
hundred and fifty years of unrequited toil
shall be sunk, and every drop of blood drawn
with the lash shall be paid by another drawn
with the sword, as was said three thousand
years ago, so still must it be said, the judg-
ments of the Lord are true and righteous
altogether."

But does the preacher wish to win the attention of the plain people? Must he not
go for his language to the gutter and the
prize-ring, or, at the very least, to the sport-
ing page of the *New York Journal?* Recently one of our eminent ministers speaking upon the Prodigal Son announced his

subject, "Home from the Hog-Pen." Surely this is the short swift path to popularity. Well, one day Lincoln said to thousands of the plain people of America, surrounded by the graves of other thousands of the plain people of America, "The world will little note, nor long remember what we say here," and then he began to utter words so pure, so lofty, that one would say he spoke the truth, that the world would indeed little note nor long remember; but for once Abraham Lincoln did not speak the truth, for those same pure and lofty words will be remembered by the plain people of America when the Civil War shall be a myth. Are all the people going to be fooled all the time?

As Lincoln speaks to us of his choice of words and his style of speech, he tells us that both have been dictated mainly by his desire to be understood. He seems to be sure that the understanding of his message will mean the acceptance of his message. A writer remarks: "He was so clear that he could not be misunderstood or misrepresented." In one of those revealing bits of autobiography Lincoln says: "I remember how, when a child, I used to get irritated when anybody talked to me in a way that I could not understand. I do not think that I ever got angry at anything else in my life,

but that always disturbed my temper and
has ever since. I am never easy now when
I am handling a thought, till I have bounded
it north, and bounded it south, and bounded
it east, and bounded it west." It is not easy
to bound on all sides the thought which the
preacher has to handle, but does not the
very difficulty of the problem bind us to
make our hearers understand?

And this leads us to listen to another consideration. As we pass from the clothes of
Lincoln's thought to the thought itself, it is
fascinating to note that our teacher would
have us always strike for what he calls " the
central idea " or " the naked issue." " That's
the naked issue, and the whole of it," he
would say. " Public opinion has a central
idea." This he must always find. " If I
can clean this case of technicalities and get
it properly swung to the jury, I'll win it."
"In law," and he might have added, in religion, "it is good policy never to plead
what you need not lest you be obliged to
prove what you cannot." " Judge Douglass," he would say, "is playing cuttlefish,
a small species of fish that has no mode of
defending itself except by throwing out a
black fluid which makes the water so dark
that the enemy cannot see it, and thus it
escapes. Is not the Judge playing the cut-

tlefish?" The foes of the common good
are expert in playing cuttlefish, and they
are never quite so happy as when we
good preachers are lost in the murk and the
dark of the unnecessary and the extraneous.
Happy the preacher who strikes for the
"central idea," the "naked issue."

We ask our teacher how in the midst of
the universal confusion and sophistry he
managed to discover the central ideas, the
naked issues. Not without immense labour
did he find them. He would walk nine miles
to get a book. The weighty volumes of
Blackstone which a stranger left in his store
in the bottom of a barrel he read. "Never
in my whole life was my mind so thoroughly
absorbed. I read until I devoured them."
Much of Lincoln's power came from his
careful statement of fact gained by hard
study. With a great price he bought his
power, and can a smaller man pay a smaller
price?

Much of our reading is a substitute for
thinking. A writer reminds us that the poet
Southey was telling a Quaker lady and with
some pride, how his time was occupied. He
studied Portuguese while he was shaving.
He studied Spanish an hour before breakfast.
He read all the forenoon, and wrote all
the afternoon. "Friend," said the Friend,

"when does thee do thy thinking?" So I hear Lincoln say to us, "Friend, let no pride of the hale fellow well met, no glory in the title of 'mixer,' vilest of all ministerial titles, lose to you the leisure for thought, the chance to make your own the central ideas, the naked issues of the faith you preach."

And now our teacher would tell us some of the inner secrets of his power as a persuader of men. One secret was his early allegiance to a great and unpopular Cause. As early as 1837 Lincoln joined with one other state representative of Illinois in signing a resolution which is said to have been the first formal declaration against the system of slavery made in any legislative body in the United States, at least west of the Hudson River. In 1849, Lincoln in Congress moved an amendment instructing the proper committee to report a bill abolishing slavery in the District of Columbia. He got hold of this thought, "Freedom is national, slavery is sectional." Just before he entered upon his duties as President, he wrote to a Southerner: "You think slavery is right, and ought to be extended, while we think it is wrong and ought to be restricted." When he became President his new position involved the primacy of a new allegiance, the allegiance to the Union. Strikingly is the change suggested by that letter to Greeley, which suggests as well every quality of the preacher's style, for which our teacher has pleaded. After certain discriminating and gently chiding words, we read, " As to the policy I seem to be pursuing, as you say, I have not meant to leave any one in doubt. I would save the Union, I would save it in the shortest way under the Constitution. If there be those who would not save the Union unless they could at the same time destroy slavery, I do not agree with them. My paramount object in this struggle is to save the Union, and is not either to save or destroy slavery. If I could save the Union without freeing any slave I would do it. And if I could save it by freeing all the slaves I would do it, and if I could do it by freeing some and leaving others slaves, I would also do that." Always indeed he knew that to further the cause of the Union was to further the cause of freedom. It was in the fall of 1862 that the two causes became inextricably united. The permanency of the Union involved the Proclamation of Emancipation.

But mark the influence of this allegiance to a Cause. At the summons of his Cause, he was perfectly willing to surrender the political promotion which he honestly openly desired. At the summons of his Cause he determined that if he failed, he would still do all he could for his Cause. One of the most pathetic pieces of literature is that private memorandum written shortly before his second election. " This morning as for some days past it seems exceedingly probable that this administration will not be reëlected. Then it will be my duty to so coöperate with the president-elect as to save the Union between the election and the inauguration, as he will have secured his election on such grounds that he cannot possibly save it afterwards." How fine it would be if a pastor looking forward to his compulsory retirement from his church could write for his guidance a memorandum like that. At the summons of his Cause, he showed an almost Christlike magnanimity. He could take into his cabinet the man who had called him the original gorilla. He could keep in his cabinet the man who had actually proposed that Lincoln should surrender to him the reins of government. He could keep in his cabinet the man who was making an active canvass for the presidency, and then when opportunity offered, he could make this man Chief Justice of the United States. At the summons of his Cause he looked, fearless, into the daily face of death. As the months passed, the pile of assassination letters grew,

but he held not his life of any account as
dear unto himself that he might fulfill his
course and the ministry assigned him by the
Cause. It is a great word of Fairbairn,
"The man who is as it were annihilated by
his mission, is most magnified by it. He
becomes an organ of deity, a voice of God."
Was Lincoln's Cause more compelling, more
imperious than that which claims our allegiance? To be Comrades of the Cause, to
know no failure but the failure of the Cause,
no triumph but the triumph of the Cause,
that is one of the great teachings of our
great teacher.

Lincoln leads us back of this fact of allegiance to a Cause to certain other charac-
teristics which make him one of the preacher's sovereign teachers. We note first his
confidence in himself. He was utterly without those bulwarks of self-respect which most
of us have. He was a very sensitive man.
He was criticized, condescended to. He was
made to wait at the door of McClellan's
headquarters. In a letter to Hackett the
actor he says, "I have endured a great deal
of ridicule without much malice and have received a great deal of kindness not quite free
from ridicule. I am used to it." When the
presidency came to him, he said in a speech
to the New York Legislature, "I trust that I

may have their assistance in piloting the ship
of state through this voyage, for if it should
suffer wreck now there will be no pilot ever
needed for another voyage." And yet knowing that he might be the last pilot of the ship,
he did not hesitate to take the helm. He
called to his assistance men whom the world
and they themselves regarded as far greater
than himself. He met diplomats, representatives of world powers, great captains with
their guns and drums, and always on terms
of perfect equality, as friends, comrades. A
minister came home after preaching his evening sermon and said to his wife, "I swear I
will never preach again." "Did any one
thank you for your sermon?" "No." "I
thought not." Garfield said of his wife, "She
is unstampedable." To have an honest self-
respect, the conviction that whatever other
men may say we have a message from God,
this is to have one of the secrets of Lincoln's
power over men. So a man speaks with authority and not as the scribes.

Along with this confidence in self, Lincoln
would lead us into his own comradeship with,
and confidence in, the people. He was called
by the one party, "Nigger, nigger-lover," by
the other party, "the slave-hound of Illinois."
His generals failed him, Congress failed him,
the papers lampooned him, yet his comrade-

ship grew into a beautiful tenderness. " Massa Linculm am eberywhere," said the negro.

" He was the north, the south, the east, the west,
　The thrall, the master, all of us in one."

And with this comradeship there was, as I have suggested, an unwavering confidence in the people. He dared to trust them, to trust us. He allowed his privacy to be invaded that he might take what he called his "weekly opinion bath." Ever he seems to be saying with Paul, "I speak as to wise men, judge ye what I say." In his first inaugural address, he asks, "Why should there not be patient confidence in the justice of the people? Is there any better or equal hope in the world?" Contrast this with the word of Carlyle to Emerson: "Beat this thing, I say, under thy dull hoofs, O dull public. Trample it and tumble it into all sinks and kennels. If thou canst kill it, kill it in God's name. If thou canst not kill it, why then, thou wilt not." A letter came recently to your desk, a letter from a minister, which breathed an absolute contempt for the people whom he served. Another letter came to your desk, a letter from a minister, which breathed a lofty condescension towards his people. Neither man can do permanent good. Keep your comradeship with the

people, your confidence in the people. So
may you become what Lincoln was, the
voice of the people when speaking their best
thoughts.

Still we have left out of account the secret
of the secrets of our teacher's power. Lincoln
had confidence in himself, he had confidence
in the people, but both these were dependent
upon his confidence in God. At first we do
not see in him any great confidence in God.
There is more of the frontier superstition.
He will not begin a journey on Friday. He
dreams, and he dreams that his dreams come
true. But as life hurls him up against its
great problems, up from superstition rises
trust. He lifts "lame hands of faith" and is
caught by the strong hand of God. Lincoln's
creed is not long, but it is the creed of his
life: "I believe in a living God." One is
reminded of Beecher's word : "I have heard
men pray 'O God of Abraham, O God
of Isaac, O God of Jacob, O God of Zion,'
but I never heard men pray 'O God of
Brooklyn, O God of America !' Why do you
not pray in the name of your father, in the
name of your mother, in the name of your
town?"

Further, would Lincoln say : "I believe in
a God who hates the wrong and loves the
right." Significant to us preachers, all, are

his words to a clergyman who expressed the hope that the Lord was on our side. "I am not at all concerned about that, for I know that the Lord is always on the side of the right, but it is my constant anxiety and prayer that I and this nation should be on the Lord's side."

> " Swiftly the politic goes: Is it dark? He
>   borrows a lantern.
> Slowly, the statesman, and sure, guiding his
>   feet by the stars."

Again he would say: "I believe in a God who answers prayer." Lincoln calls upon his people again and again to join him in petition. He is deeply grateful to know that they are praying for him. He says of himself, "I have often been driven to my knees by the overwhelming conviction that I had nowhere else to go. My own wisdom and the wisdom of all about me seemed insufficient for the day."

Another word of his creed is this: "I believe in a God who is a loving heavenly Father." I know that the letter is more familiar to you than to me: but I should wrong you if I did not read it to you once more; a letter whose almost unmatched English but expresses the perfectness of his trust in our Father.

Executive Mansion,
Washington, Nov. 21, 1864.

To Mrs. Bixby,
     Boston, Mass.

Dear Madam :—I have been shown in the files of the War Department a statement of the Adjutant General of Massachusetts that you are the mother of five sons who have died gloriously on the field of battle. I feel how weak and fruitless must be any word of mine which should attempt to beguile you from the grief of a loss so overwhelming. But I cannot refrain from tendering you the consolation that may be found in the thanks of the republic they died to save. I pray that our heavenly Father may assuage the anguish of your bereavement, and leave you only the cherished memory of the loved and lost, and the solemn pride that must be yours to have laid so costly a sacrifice upon the altar of freedom.

Yours very sincerely and respectfully,

A. Lincoln.

Till his little boy died, he seems never to have given much hopeful thought to immortality ; but then through the guidance of a friend, he was led to add one more word to his creed : "I believe in the life everlasting." In his creed is no word which bespeaks the necessity of uniting with the visible church. Our preachers had not yet learned to strike for the central ideas, the naked issues. But through all his life he was accustomed to attend church. Always he kept in close touch with the churches. Earnestly he sought their coöperation. Again and again he thanked them for the gifts of love and of life which they had offered to the country. I have not the slightest doubt that were he alive to-day he would be found among those bound formally as well as vitally to the Christian Church.

But I think that at the last our teacher would lay his great friendly hand upon the shoulder of each one of us, his pupils, and would say, "One thing, one thing is needful. Have faith in God."

It is true that Lincoln's faith did not make him the radiant Christian of whom we dream. A writer speaks of "that abiding melancholy, that painful sense of the incompleteness of life which had been his mother's dowry." In his last ride with his wife he said, "We must both try to be more cheerful in the future. Between the war and the loss of our darling boy, we have been very miserable." But after all, he was one

> "Who never doubted clouds would break,
>   Never dreamed, though right were worsted,
>   wrong would triumph,
>   Held we fall to rise, are baffled to fight better,
>   sleep to wake."

You remember the story that Dr. A. J. Lyman tells us of Beecher. The two were coming from some scene of funeral solemnity. "Well, Lyman," said Beecher, "I suppose they will try to take me out to Greenwood some day, but God knows I shan't stay there." "Where shall we look for you then, Mr. Beecher?" "Somewhere in the midst of things fighting for my country." So I love to think of him who has been our teacher, as somewhere in the midst of things, still fighting for his country, and teaching us to fight the better, with persuasive words chosen from the armoury of the common speech, welded with exceeding care into weapons directed straight to the hearts, the wills of men. I think of him as teaching us rather to ally ourselves with the cause of the world-wide civilization of brotherly men, to confide anew in our noblest selves, in our fellow men, in our fathers' God, in our own God. More willingly I think of that incident which occurred at the close of the war. Lincoln was passing through Richmond. An old coloured mammy held high in air a little sick white child: "Look at de saviour, honey; touch the hem of his garment, honey, and yuh pain will be done gone." I think of Lincoln as our nation's saviour, through whose healing virtue a nation's agony was assuaged, a nation's saviour, who would teach each of us in his own place to be in some sense a saviour of mankind.

" Admire heroes if thou wilt," says one, "but only admire and thou remainest a slave. Learn their secret, to commit thyself to God, and to obey Him, and thou shalt become a hero too."

V

The Preacher and His Master

V

THE PREACHER AND HIS MASTER

THE Master looks forward to the day of universal empire, to the time when His personality shall dominate human life. The words which the fourth Gospel puts into His lips express the certain conviction of His heart: "I, if I be lifted up from the earth, will draw all men unto myself." He says to a little group of fishermen, "Ye are the salt of the earth, ye are the light of THE WORLD." Jesus expects His kingdom to be not only universal but eternal. Though the world empires become as the chaff of the summer threshing floor, His kingdom shall be an everlasting kingdom, and His dominion, one that shall not pass away.

And yet—the fact would strike us as amazing if it were not a commonplace of our religion,—Jesus expects to win this empire, universal and eternal, by an appeal to men. From the wilderness to Golgotha, Jesus steadfastly refuses to use force in the extension and establishment of His kingdom. He will hypnotize no man, He will break down no man's doors. "Behold I stand at the door and knock." Nor will He use the men and the means of Cæsar. The apologists for war have reminded us of Jesus' cleansing of the temple as an instance of His use of force; but surely the whip of small cords and the overturning of the money changers' tables were but the symbols of that zeal for Jehovah's house which consumed His spirit. He does say, "I came not to bring peace but a sword." But it is the exegesis of an insane asylum which would at this place put a literal sword into the hand of the follower of Jesus. The sword is the symbol of division. If a literal sword should by any possibility be intended, it is fairly clear that the sword would be wielded not by Jesus' friends but by His foes. His friends are not to conquer by murder. They are to conquer by martyrdom. At the last supper, we hear the disciples strenuously discussing material preparedness : " Lord, here are two swords." Two swords, forsooth, to defend thirteen men ! " It is enough," said Jesus. " I have been with you so long, but still you do not understand me." " Let him sell his cloak and buy a sword ": what does that mean ? " Thus far you have been sheep, following me, the good shepherd. Thus far you have been children, following me, as

Friend. Now I am to leave you. Now you are to have another temper, that of the soldier, who girds his sword upon his thigh ; you are to march out with the weapons of grace and truth to meet and master the world." When in the Garden poor Peter, ill practiced with the sword, cuts off the ear rather than the head of the servant of the high priest, what does Jesus say ? "Put up again thy sword into its place, for all they that take the sword shall perish with the sword."

Is not that a suggestive story told by Silvester Horne ? A little boy had received as a Christmas present a toy sword, with which throughout the day he killed great numbers of imaginary soldiers. Towards evening, his mother began to speak quietly to him of the meaning of the coming of Jesus, spoke of the life of love and tenderness and sacrifice, until at last the little face grew serious and thoughtful, and the boy said, "Mother, I think I will hide my sword. I shouldn't like Jesus to see it."

A Christian nation can get no aid or comfort from Jesus, as she goes to war, unless she is able to convince herself that her war is a corollary in action of the teaching of Jesus, in which He summarizes the law and the prophets: "Thou shalt love the Lord thy God, Thou shalt love thy neighbour as thyself." No nation which claims to be Christian can go to war, unless her citizens are able honestly to declare before the world in the presence of God, "We love the Lord our God, we love our neighbour nation as ourselves; therefore we go against our neighbour nation with aeroplanes and superdreadnaughts and submarines, and infinite munitions and asphyxiating gases. Our guns are expressions in steel of the grace and truth which we as followers of Jesus are alone permitted to use." Does that mean that we can never go to war? I do not say that, but I do say that any honest obedience to the word of Jesus would have made impossible most of the wars of the world, with "their mud and blood and blasphemy." No Christian nation could possibly make her own the slogan, "Remember the Maine." Had we been a Christian nation, our only conceivable battle cry in Cuba would have been, "Rescue the Perishing."

As men then who would preach Christ, let us ask ourselves: What is the appeal of Jesus? That is: To what motives does Jesus appeal? Negatively we may say, Jesus does not appeal to the very natural desire of men for the sensational, the spectacular. He will not win men by the asceticism of the Baptist. He will walk and talk and

eat and drink with men, a friendly man.
He will win no man by the duplication of the
mysteries of Eleusis. "Come and See, Come
and See." His very miracles, which were
but the inevitable outflow of the compassion
and power of His personality, brought to
Him a notoriety which embarrassed and ham-
pered His real work. The multitudes would
have followed with a glad heart a Messiah
who should suddenly drop from the pinnacle
of the temple into the temple court. Deliberately He rejects the rôle of the wonder-
monger. "No sign shall be given to this
generation, but the sign of Jonah." The
sign seekers belong to a prolific race, but
Jesus to-day as yesterday is singularly unre-
sponsive to their demands. "He shall not
cry nor lift up nor cause his voice to be heard
in the street." He will come into the lives
of men as the night mist comes upon the
grass, as the spring time comes upon the
world.

Again Jesus does not appeal to the very
natural desire of men for a present paradise
of sensuous blessedness or material well-being. He is no Demas luring earth's pilgrims
to his silver mine. He has no sympathy
with that ancient, modern code of ethics
which declares that a man must live, which
proclaims that it is better for a man to steal

than to starve. " If any man would come after me, let him deny himself, and take up his cross daily and follow me," and starve if the need come, yes, and let all his family starve, if the need come. " The time is at hand when he that killeth you will think that he doeth God service." One of His startling parables pictures to us a certain rich man who had won his paradise of sensuous blessedness and went to sleep, who woke to find himself a fool. " Come to our church. We have the finest organ, the most delicious music, the most elegant and eloquent preacher in town. Come, be a citizen of the kingdom of God. Haven't you noticed that the ablest, most prominent, most successful business men in our town are Christians? Be good and you will be a welcome guest at the bank. Haven't you observed that the captains of our football teams for seven years have all been Christians?" I miss such words from the appeal of Jesus.

Nor does Jesus appeal to any narrowing self-centered desire to escape from a future hell and to win a paradise of spiritual blessedness or immaterial well-being. Jesus did regard the life here and the life hereafter as of one piece. We see a freshman going wrong, and we say to him, " My dear fellow, see where you are going. You are losing,

losing, losing until at last YOU will be lost."
Jesus bade men look whither they were
going, nor could He speak as a teacher who
believed that the path ended in the blind
alley of the grave. Jesus used the religious
terminology of His people, its words speaking
of rewards and punishments; but the holiness motivated by a selfish fear of hell, or by a
selfish desire for heaven would be unholy, it
would be smirched. Such holiness has no
heritage in the heaven of Jesus; it is the pos-
session of the man who, as one says, " put-
ters around in his own petty self-made hell."
In St. Louis a while ago I saw a sign painted
on the windows of a mission, "Holiness or
Hell." In Ashtabula I saw the announce-
ment of a sermon, " Eternity, Where?"
There is a way of preaching heaven and hell,
which leads one to sympathize with the
woman of long ago who went through the
streets of Alexandria, with a torch in one
hand and a pitcher of water in the other, and
who cried, "I would burn up heaven with
this torch, and extinguish hell with this
water, that man might love God for Himself
alone."

At the very outset Jesus would seem to
ignore those motives by which alone He
might hope successfully to appeal to men.
Indeed the crowds do turn from Him. The

soldiers adorn Him with an old purple robe. Pilate writes in the languages of the world the inscription for the cross: "This is the king of the Jews," and a roar of laughter in the prætorium follows this sharp sally of Roman wit.

To what motives does Jesus appeal? Positively, Jesus appeals to the universal desire of men for the knowledge of God, for friendship with God. To know God, to know God: this has been the desire of the nations and of the ages. "Religion," says Fairbairn, "is so essential to man that he cannot escape from it. It besets him, penetrates him, holds him even against his will." A German critic has remarked, "Religion is the most pernicious malady of humanity." It is a persistent divine disease of men. Now and then you do come across one of those farmers of Thoreau who would carry their God to market if they could get anything for Him. Now and then you come across one of those monstrous fishers of men and of nations who sacrifice unto their own nets, and burn incense unto their own drags. Once in a while you meet with one of those psychologists who "cannot persuade themselves that divine personal beings, be they primitive gods or the Christian Father, have more than a subjective existence." Occasionally you see men who go about the world proclaiming how little they believe, as if somehow their infidelity lifted them to summits of thought and wisdom above those on which walked Isaiah and Paul and Jesus. But one always feels that such men have never tasted life, or else are deceiving their own souls. They speak more truly who say with Mæterlinck, "It is only by the communications we have with the Infinite that we are to be distinguished from each other." Walt Whitman speaks for the race when he uses those words which we all know and love :

" A noiseless patient spider
  I marked, where on a little promontory it
    stood isolated,
  Marked how to explore the vacant vast sur-
    rounding,
  It launched forth filament, filament, filament,
    out of itself,
  Ever unreeling them, ever tirelessly speeding
    them.

" And you, O my soul, where you stand,
  Surrounded, detached, in measureless oceans
    of space,
  Ceaselessly musing, venturing, throwing, seek-
    ing the spheres to connect them
  Till the bridge you will need be formed, till the
    ductile anchor hold,
  Till the gossamer thread you fling catch some-
    where, O my soul."

To know God! Wherever in all the world a man has been found who seemed to know anything about God, that man has been hated, it may be, loved, it may be: that man has always been followed.

Now the fundamental postulate of Christianity—perhaps the words are another's—is this, that God can be known; and the second postulate of Christianity I take to be this, that God can be known as a friend. In all lands and times, friendship with deity has been regarded as beatitude. Does God see and know and care for us? "Come unto me," says Jesus, "and I will make you to know God. I will make you to know God as your friend, as your Father. He is your Father. You may become in a new sense his Child. Come unto me: I am the way, I am the way from the meanest man, the most ignorant man, the most degraded man, straight to the Father's home and the Father's heart." When the Danish missionaries were translating the Word, they came to the passage which reads, "They shall be called sons of God." The native amanuensis laid down his pen: "Missionary, this is too much. Let me write it: 'They shall be permitted to kiss His feet.'" Nay, they shall be called sons of God. And I say to you that wherever you can find an honest man who has dug his way

down the least distance beneath the surface
of life, there you find a man who answers
back, "Master, canst Thou do it? Canst
Thou make me to know God as my friend,
as my Father? Then Thou wilt draw me to
Thee, and hold me fast to Thee forever."

And this leads me to speak of a second
appeal of our Master. Jesus appeals to the
universal desire of men for a man's life. Even
where the great religious teachers have taught
that the goal of life is a ceaseless dreamless
sleep, the human heart has rebelled, and insisted that it is life, not death, it is life and
fuller that we want. But a man's life! What
does that mean? Think it through. A man's
life. What is needful that a man should live
a man's life? That a man may live a man's life,
the forces which now tend to impoverish life
must themselves positively enrich life. What
forces tend to impoverish life? "Well," one
will say, "sickness, poverty itself, the ebb and
flow, the ups and downs of circumstance."
You remember the word of Rosebury speaking of Napoleon on St. Helena, "For six
years he tasted the bitterness of slow, re-
morseful, desolate death." The tragedy is
not less real, when it is less conspicuous.
Often in the great city, one sees a man
who has given himself body and soul to a
certain business. The business has been

undermined by the rapid economic changes of the years. And the man's hands are empty, his heart is shrivelled. He is poor. Then there is bereavement. Do you happen to know the derivation of the word Bereavement? I have been told that it roots in an Anglo-Saxon word which means to steal, to plunder, to rob. When our friends go from us we say that we are bereaved, literally, plundered, robbed, despoiled. Though we may hope to make life longer and safer, though we may dare dream of the time when the inhabitant shall not say, " I am sick," yet no man can claim exemption from life's changes; but if a man is to live a MAN'S life, these changes which so often impoverish must actually enrich life.

Perhaps more impoverishing is the deadly and meaningless monotony of life. A letter came the other day to a preacher friend of mine : " At the next morning service, will you have a special message for those whose vision is dimming and whose hold on God is slipping under the pressure not of great bereavement, but of steadily grinding care and responsibility ? Perhaps you have met such a situation. At all events you seem to have learned the secret of a vital steadying relationship with God. You have already helped me, and I beg your further help before everything goes, and the bitterness already creeping in overmasters me. I despise anonymous letters, but remain, A troubled parishioner." We try at times to amuse ourselves with fool's gold, to avoid the meaningless monotony by an equally meaningless " acceleration." We know in our hearts that we are not living a man's life ; we are poor.

If a man is to live a man's life, the forces which now tend to destroy life must themselves be destroyed. Then sin must be killed out of a man. I suspect that there is to-day a decline of the sense of sin. A preacher tells me, " In Cleveland, I don't meet men who regard themselves as sinners." But men know very well that they are the victims of the divided self. At the desk of the city business man is a telephone, and he may be called up by the Salvation Army or the grill room, by the gambling hell or the Society for the Prevention of Cruelty to Children. They may be on the wire at the same time. Isn't it true ? A letter, a bit of sunshine, a fit of depression, a word of gossip, and lo, the friend, or the scholar, or the libertine, or the pessimist within a man calls him up and at times all these personalities will seem to be struggling within him to get a hearing. We do not speak much of sin, we call it by all sorts of pretty names, but still there are hosts of men who share the longing of Kipling's pilgrim, who came to the curator of the museum at Lahore with his story of the River of the Arrow: "Where Buddha's arrow fell, there broke out a stream, which presently became a river, whose nature by our Lord's beneficence is that whoso bathes in it washes away every taint and speckle of sin. Where is that river, Fountain of Wisdom, where fell the arrow? Surely thou dost know. See, I am an old man. I ask with my head between thy feet, O fountain of wisdom. We know he drew the bow. We know the arrow fell. We know the stream gushed. Where then is the river? My dream told me to find it. So I came. I am here, but where is the river?" Where is the river in which a man may cleanse away every taint and speckle of sin? The nations do not know. Mr. Mott says, "I have asked the students of forty different nations to show me any power except Christ that could save their life from sin, and give them strength. Only one young man ever claimed knowledge of such a power. I said to him, 'I am glad to meet you. Come with me, and give your message to the young men of the world. I need your help.' That same evening that young man came to me and said that he was a slave of sin, and the

power of which he spoke, his own will, had
not been able to save him."

If, in order that one may live a man's life,
the forces now tending to destroy life must be
destroyed, then death must be put to death.
Don't you think that death is a pretty shabby
ending of a man's life? "A beautiful ad-
venture"? Yes, if death is not death. I
talked a while ago with an old friend of mine.
I said, "How tall are you?" "Well," said
he, "I used to be six feet, two and a half. I
am not that any more. I am not six feet
any more." Isn't that pathetic? So we
shrivel and shrivel until our grave clothes
fit us.

"The phenomenon of consciousness ceases
with the death of the cerebral cells." How
lightly we say over the words. Think what
they mean. Do you recall that letter of
Huxley to Morley?

4 Marlboro Place, N. W.,
December 30, 1883.

My dear Morley:
    All our good wishes to you and yours.
The great thing one has to wish for as time
goes on is vigour as long as life lasts, and
death as soon as vigour flags. It is a curious
thing that I find my dislike of the thought
of extinction increasing as I get older and
nearer the goal. It flashes across me at all
sorts of times with a sort of horror that in

1900 I shall probably know no more of what is going on than I did in 1800. I had sooner be in hell a good deal, at any rate in one of the upper circles, where the climate and company are not too trying. I wonder if you are plagued in this way.

Ever yours,
T. H. H.

In his book, "Facts and Comments," Herbert Spencer says, "It seems a strange and repugnant conclusion that with the cessation of consciousness at death, there ceases to be any knowledge of having existed." I grant that there are times, tired times, when nothing seems so desirable as a long sleep, but even then the thought of the extinction of our loved ones seems unspeakably horrible. Omar of course has an easy answer to all our questionings.

> " Would you be happy? Hearken then the way.
> Heed not to-morrow, heed not yesterday.
> The magic words of life are here and now.
> O fools, that after some to-morrow stray."

That is, put your memory to sleep, put your hope to sleep, and then be happy like a dog or like a cat, but not like a man. If a man is going to live a man's life, then death must be put to death, or life, as the universe itself, is indeed God's great joke, rather a jest perpetrated by some Caliban of a god. "What must I do to inherit eternal life?" The cry of the rich young man is echoed by every man worthy the name of a man. The rich young man did not wish "a ladylike tea-party elysium, where there is a tedious cooing of bliss from everybody." He was not seeking "sugar plums" for himself. He was seeking LIFE. He might have gone to the rabbis of his own people, he might have gone to the stoics of Rome, he might have gone to the pundits of the East. Their best philosophies would have taught him to obey an impossible law, to endure an unendurable life, to get free from the wheel of things. Alone, unique, among the teachers of the world, our Master speaks to men, "Come unto me and I will give you LIFE. I will give you the real, the rich, the abounding, the eternal life." And again I say, wherever you can find an honest man, who has dug down beneath the surface of existence, there you find a man who answers back, "Master, canst Thou do it? Canst Thou give me a man's life? Then 'of all mankind I cleave to Thee, and to Thee will I cleave alway.'"

Again, there is a third appeal of Jesus, which cannot be logically separated from the others. Jesus appeals to the universal desire of men for leadership, a leadership other than their own.

We have often observed the longing of men for a king. Far back in the days of the Judges Israel longed for a king. A little while ago, one of the countries of Europe was scouring the continent to find a king. What we see in the realm of politics, we see in the realm of science. In an Ohio university there is an eminent surgeon whose students call him "the king," and they follow him with a devotion as eager as was ever that of the soldiers of the Little Corporal. What we see in the realm of science we see in the realm of religion. The devotion of the Moslem to Mohammed, of the Hindu to Krishna, the devotion of the Mormon to Joseph Smith, of the Christian Scientist to Mrs. Eddy, these are all the expressions of the desire for a king. And this desire is by no means a maudlin sentiment. I hold it to be the kingliest quality of men. Your little woman whose chief interests are low necks and high teas thinks she has no need of a king. But let her live a while. Your great woman, your Frances Willard, your Harriet Beecher Stowe, needs a king. Your ordinary woman who for one half-hour has looked out into that world in which to-day breaker boys are taking in dust and death

with the same breath, that world in which
to-day the seamstress sews a double thread,
a shroud as well as a shirt, that world in
which little children are sent barefooted
out into the night, while their fathers shoot
each other to death and call war glorious,
that woman needs a king.   I was struck by
the word of Jane Carlyle, who confessed
that she had a devil inside her which was
always bidding her March, March, but which
burst into laughter when she asked where
she was to march to.

Your little man, a chip on the face of the
waters, thinks he doesn't need a king.   Let
him live a little while and he will learn his
need.

> " Last night my soul drove out to sea,
>   Down through the pagan gloom,
>   As chartless as eternity,
>   As dangerous as doom.

> " By blinding gusts of no-god chased,
>   My crazy craft plunged on.
>   I crept aloft in prayer to find
>   The lighthouse of the dawn.

> " No shore, no star, no sail ahead,
>   No lookout's saving song,
>   Death and the rest athwart my bow,
>   And all my reckoning wrong."

Meanwhile your great man, your Lincoln,
your Gladstone, needs a king.   Your ordi-

nary man who has stood for one half-hour gazing into that stupendous melting pot of God, in which we are bidden see the races and the nations fusing and reforming,—he needs a king, some one on whose throne steps he may kneel and bow obeisance, some great commander in whose comradeship he may be strong.

Never was the desire for leadership so imperious as at this hour. We are tasting the ripe fruits of the industrial development of the last thirty years, and those fruits taste of human blood. We are tasting the unripe fruits of a recent industrial development, with its forced growth, and again the fruits taste of human blood. The public square of the great city is lined with benches, and the benches are filled with drunks and bums, and the great city like the Roman matron of old must say, " These are my jewels." Now " ascetic Christianity," says Rauschenbusch, " found the world evil and left it. The times call for a revolutionary Christianity that shall find the world evil and change it." Yes, and whether Christians or not, men want to change it. Did you notice the remark of Lyman Abbott? He said, " For some ten years I have been giving myself to preaching among collegians, and in all that time I have never been asked the question, What

must I do to be saved? But many times
have I been asked, What must I do to save
others?" Certain it is that the passion for
saving others burns white hot within the
hearts of manly men to-day.

> " Sometimes with a rush the intolerable craving
> Shivers throughout me like a trumpet call.
> Oh, to save these, to perish for their saving,
> Die for their life, be offered for them all."

Yes, but how to save these? One doesn't
exactly like to "run the hazard of his life
against a hen-roost." How by death to win
life for others? How to make a sacrifice not
only complete but completely serviceable?
You recall the Chicago saloon-keeper who
speaking of a recent anti-saloon agitation
said, "This is no Willy-Hold-the-Baby
proposition. This is hell." The job which
faces men to-day is no job for nursemaids,
male or female; it is for us to extinguish
hell. But how? All about us are fakirs
with their patent fire extinguishers telling us
how to put out the fire. The only trouble
with them is, they can't do it. Some years
ago, Jesus said to a couple of fishermen,
" Come ye after me and I will make you
fishers of men." A little later to a larger
group, He said, "Go ye and make disciples
of all the nations, and lo, I am with you all
the days, even unto the consummation of the

age." And down through the years, the
preacher's Master has been calling to men,
" Come unto me and I will be your leader.
I will lead you into a life of power, a life
strong to climb towards God, a life strong to
stoop and bear the burdens of your brothers,
a life strong to sway and strong to serve the
world." And once more I say, wherever
you can find a man in whom any manhood
survives, a man who has worked his way
down beneath the mere surface of life, there
you find a man who answers back to Jesus,
" Master, canst Thou do it ? Canst Thou be
my leader ? Then I will follow Thee 'through
heaven and hell, the earth, the sea and the
air.' "

Does Jesus appeal to these universal desires of men to thwart them ? After the instruction of the centuries it is but a truism to
say that Jesus appeals to these desires of men
to satisfy them with a sublime fulfillment.
Men longing for the knowledge of God, for
friendship with God, have placed their hands
in the hand of Jesus and have felt the pressure of the heavenly Father's hand. Men
whose lives have been one long struggle for
life have tasted of Him the living bread and
have never hungered any more. Through
the desert of the years pilgrims have sought

and in Jesus they have found the fountain of living waters, and no man who has drunk of that fountain has ever thirsted any more. There has risen within him a fountain springing up unto eternal life. "Jesus," says Brooks, "was not so much the deed doer or the word sayer; He was rather the life giver." Such He has ever been. Through Him men have come to live a life of such a character that its cessation would proclaim the world a madhouse. Men have come to Jesus seeking leadership. They have entered a sad world, but wherever they have followed Jesus they have turned sorrow into joy. They have come into an impure world, but wherever they have placed their feet in the footprints of Jesus there have grown the flowers of domestic purity. They have come into a cruel world, a world which delighted to see ten thousand gladiators contend for life in the arena. Wherever they have followed Jesus they have transformed cruelty into mercy.

It was my privilege to be in Toronto at the dedication of the glorious pile of buildings known as Knox College, the Presbyterian theological school connected with the University. As we sat in the Gothic chapel and listened to words of faith and hope and love, almost constantly through the half open windows we could hear the sharp commands of sergeants drilling their awkward squads of boys. Two hundred, three hundred, four hundred, they marched across the campus back and forth hour after hour. Why? That they might all too possibly die in the wild war. But in the addresses, this thought was expressed again and again : The peace which must at last close this war will be the signal for a greater, madder war, in which shall be involved not only the United States but the entire Orient, if, if that peace is not made in accordance with the principles of Jesus Christ. This I profoundly believe. A friend of mine was telling us of a picture in the Metropolitan Museum of Art in New York. It represents the Crusaders come at last to the holy city, the goal of their desires. Below them shine the domes and minarets of Jerusalem. Not an eye is turned thither. Rather every eye is turned towards the heavens, where in vision is seen Jesus Christ, who has led them all the way. And to this day, wherever you meet crusaders who have actually achieved the rescue of any quarter of the captive city, there you find men who consciously or unconsciously have followed Jesus Christ, our Master.

Had Jesus used the weapons of physical conquest He would never have conquered human hearts. Those words of Chunder

Sen uttered in 1879 still speak the truth:
"Who rules India? It is neither diplomacy
nor the bayonet which sways our hearts.
Armies never won the heart of a nation, and
you cannot deny that our hearts are touched,
are won, are overwhelmed by a higher power,
and that power is Christ. Christ rules British
India, not the British government. None but
Jesus, none but Jesus, none, I say, but Jesus,
ever deserved this bright diadem, and Jesus
shall have it." Had Jesus sought the sensational, the spectacular, He would never have
appealed to the wise; had He appealed to the
desire for ease, He would never have appealed
to heroes. Jesus knew what was in man,
dared to bide His time, dared to appeal to
those motives which beneath all that segre-
gates us, colour, race, money, national an-
tipathies, still rule the hearts of men. Into
the inner realms of life, the preacher's Master
enters, sure that the day will come when He
shall be acknowledged King.

May I speak then to the Master's preachers? Shall not the appeal of Jesus come to
us with resistless compulsion? May we not
count ourselves among those for whom Cuth-
bert Hall speaks as he addresses the men of
the East: "Educated men of the West hold
the faith of Christ not as a fragile treasure to

be guarded against the rough onslaughts of unbelief, but as a mighty impregnable fortress against which the gates of hell shall not prevail"?

And the Master's preacher has no other task than this, to voice the appeal of Jesus. Woe to us if we are guilty of the charge made against us that we are "sellers of rhetoric." Ours to proclaim a living God, whom men may love, an eternal life which men may live, a leader whom men may trust, a living way if you please, which men may follow to the journey's end.

How then shall we preachers voice the appeal of Jesus? By our words. This of course. The thought that we are simply voicing the appeal of Jesus will keep us from all scolding, from all pulpit smartnesses, from all assumption, from all dogmatism. A minister may say almost anything to his people if they know that his words are the pleading of a great Christlike love.

Again we shall voice the appeal of Jesus, like Jesus Himself, by our works. Gesta Christi, the deeds of Christ, speak a language which the men of every tongue understand. As we listen to a great preacher, we think, "Oh, if we only had his voice, his piercing glance, his brains, his immense and available learning, which he wears as lightly as a flower." And then we think of that letter of Fitzgerald: "Oh, this wonderful, wonderful world, and we who stand in the middle of it are in a maze, except poor Mathews of Bedford, who fixes his eyes upon a wooden Cross and has no misgiving whatsoever. When I was at his chapel on Good Friday, he called at the end of his grand sermon on some of the people to say merely this, that they believed Christ had redeemed them; and first one got up, and in sobs declared that she believed it; and then another, and then another—I was quite overset—all poor people: how much richer than all who fill London churches!" You remember Jehovah's word to Ezekiel, "Thou art unto them as a very lovely song of one that hath a pleasant voice, and can play well on an instrument, for they hear thy words, but they do them not." How often men listen to the eloquent preacher as to a skilled musician who fills an hour with a pleasing song, but stirs no soul to action. On the other hand there are men who like Moses were neither eloquent before Jehovah spake to them, nor after the vision of Jehovah, but by their deeds have spoken the language of compelling appeal.

We think, "Oh, if we could only be great city preachers." And then we get such a word as this: "In Boston it was recently revealed that about eighty per cent. of the pastors and Christian workers of the four leading denominations of the city were born and reared in the country." What does that mean? For one thing it means this : that in quiet country places disciples of Jesus have stood beside the cross, preaching with the words of the pulpit, yes, but rather with the more effective speech of the day's work, so that lads going up to college and down to the city have not forgotten, but have begun in their turn to voice the appeal of Jesus.

I knew two preachers. One of them had rare felicity of utterance, an extraordinary skill in exegesis. Sunday after Sunday he voiced the appeal of Jesus, but day after day as he walked the streets in silence he preached a sermon that shouted down the message of his Master. The other man had no felicity of utterance, no skill in exegesis. He had a singular inability to get his message, as our boys say, over the desk. But day by day as he walked the streets, women pointed him out to their husbands, "There is a holy man of God, who passeth by us continually." Little children loved to meet him ; and the simple fact is this, that the daily sermon of that preacher's life transfigured the sermon of the Sabbath, and on the Sabbath men listened to him as once in Antioch or Constantinople men listened to John of the Golden Mouth.

A certain woman broke an alabaster box, and poured the precious ointment upon the feet of Christ. Nineteen hundred years have passed, and the fragrance of that ointment has filled every apartment in the vast house which shelters Christendom. Her quiet deed has preached a sermon to the generations. The hands which bear the stigmata have indeed singular power to call men to " the Lord of Calvary."

But men have followed Jesus not alone for what He said and did, but for what He was. And He is the first born among many brethren. As we preachers, brethren of the Master, seek to voice His appeal, we shall fulfill our calling most effectively by the silent speech of character. When my friend Harlan P. Beach was walking along a street in China, he chanced to overhear one Chinese speak to a friend, " There goes Jesus." It has been said that men came ostensibly to hear Rutherford but really to see Jesus. I asked a friend regarding a certain minister : " Do you count him a strong man ? " " If you mean a bright man, yes : if you mean a spiritual man, no." In some real sense we must eat the flesh and drink the blood of the Son of Man. In some real fashion the life of Christ must enter ours, so that to us to live shall be Christ.

"Ideas," says George Eliot, "are often poor ghosts. Our sun-filled eyes cannot discern them—they pass athwart us in their vapour, and cannot make themselves felt. But sometimes they are made flesh, they breathe upon us with warm breath, they touch us with soft responsive hands, they look at us with sad sincere eyes, and speak to us in appealing tones; they are clothed in a living human soul, with all its conflicts, its faith and its love. Then their presence is a power, then they shake us like a passion, and we are drawn after them with gentle compulsion, as flame is drawn to flame." As the ideas of Jesus are clothed in our human souls, may we gain the ultimate power of the preacher, a power which can never be monopolized by the preachers whom the world calls wise and mighty and noble.

Shall our Master's appeal, as we give it, be effective? Grant that we may not succeed. If by the language of our words, our deeds, our characters, we have voiced that appeal, we can say with Paul, "I am pure from the blood of all men. If any man commits soul murder or soul suicide, I am not responsible." Shall the appeal be effective? Not with every man; any more than in the days when Jesus lived with Judas, loved him, lost him. Nor yet may the appeal of Jesus be successful in every company known as a church of Jesus Christ. The word may be true, " The church must be a much smaller thing before it can be a bigger."

But the world is going Jesus' way. Men have not believed it. They have trusted the minutes against the centuries ; but the world is going Jesus' way, and the man who is against Jesus has the universe against him. The man who is on the side of Jesus, and with limitless confidence voices His appeal to men, that man may seem to walk a very lonely way : he is in the current of events, strong in their strength ; the universe is on his side.

So I would close these studies, using the words which Jones of Haverford taught me, words with which we may address those who discount our ideals :

" Dreamers of dreams ?   We take the taunt with
        gladness,
    Knowing that God beyond the years you see
    Hath wrought the dreams that count with you
        for madness
    Into the substance of the life to be."

The preacher's Master will not permit the preacher's hope to be put to shame.

Printed in the United States of America

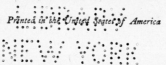

STUART NYE HUTCHISON   *Pastor First Presbyterian Church, Norfolk, Va.*

The Soul of a Child

Five-Minute Sermons to Children. Net $1.00.

Here is a volume of talks to children, well worth while, the talks are *really* to children and not simply so-called. The author has the gift of being able to select a really interesting theme, of treating it befittingly and has moreover, that rare faculty of knowing when and where to leave off in the matter of application.

OTIS TIFFANY BARNES

Children's Object Story-Sermons

12mo, cloth, net 75c.

"Objects of common every-day usage are employed as texts from which helpful lessons, adapted to little children are drawn. Cannot fail to be of practical service to all having occasion to address children."—*Heidelberg Teacher.*

WALTER RUSSELL BOWIE, D.D.   *St. Paul's P. E. Church Richmond*

The Children's Year

Fifty-two Five Minute Talks to Children. Introduction by Dr. Henry Sloane Coffin. Cloth, net $1.00.

"Few men have shown greater gifts in preaching to children than the writer. The value of these sermons as helps to parents and Sunday School teachers, and as suggestions to ministers, will be at once apparent."—*Henry Sloane Coffin, D.D.*

ANNUAL S. S. LESSON HELPS

By MARTHA TARBELL, Ph. D.

Tarbell's Teachers' Guide

to the International Sunday School Lessons. 8vo, cloth, net $1.15 (postpaid $1.25).

Dr. J. H. Jowett says: "Of very great service to Sunday school teachers."

THE POPULAR LESSON HELP

The Practical Commentary

on the International Sunday School Lessons. Cloth, net 50c (postpaid 60c).

R. A. TORREY, D.D.

The Gist of the Lesson

A Commentary on the International S. S. Lessons. 16mo. flexible cloth, net 25c.

SERMONS AND ADDRESSES

J. H. JOWETT, D.D.   *Fifth Avenue Presbyterian Church*
New York

The Whole Armour of God

12mo, cloth, net $1.35.

"This popular preacher is, not only by his own people, but also by large numbers of others, considered the very greatest preacher. He is possessed of a rare and perhaps unequalled combination of the very qualities which captivate. His thoughts are always expressed in the simplest possible diction, so that their crystalline clearness makes them at once apprehended."—*Christian Evangelist.*

EDGAR DE WITT JONES   *Author of "The Inner Circle"*

The Wisdom of God's Fools

And Other Sermons. 12mo, cloth, net $1.15.

A volume of discourses, displaying the same facility for the right word and fitting phrase which marked the author's previous work. Mr. Jones preaches sermons that *read* well—a not at all common quality. He is a thinker too; and brings to his thinking a lucidity and attractiveness which make his presentation of great truths an artistic, as well as an inspiring achievement. A note of deep spirituality is everywhere manifest.

FREDERICK F. SHANNON   *Pastor of the Reformed-Church-on-the-Heights, Brooklyn, N. Y.*

The Enchanted Universe

And Other Sermons. 12mo, cloth, net $1.00.

Mr. Shannon's reputation as an eloquent and forceful preacher is still further enhanced by his new volume of sermons. The fervid, glowing character of the popular Brooklyn pastor's appeals, make the reading of his latest book, not only an inspiring, but a fascinating exercise.

GEORGE W. TRUETT, D.D.   *Pastor First Baptist*
Church, Dallas, Tex.

We Would See Jesus and Other Sermons

Compiled and edited by J. B. Cranfill. Net $1.15.

"One of the greatest—many would say the greatest—of all the world's preachers to-day. It ranks high among the extant books of sermons, past and present, and deserves a place in millions of homes."—*Biblical Recorder.*

BISHOP CHARLES EDWARD CHENEY

A Neglected Power

And Other Sermons. 12mo, cloth, net $1.00.

"Thoroughly evangelical in spirit, refreshing in Biblical truth and abounding in helpful ministrations for every day life."—*Evangelical Messenger.*

LEWIS SPERRY CHAFER

The Kingdom in History and Prophecy

Introduction by C. I. Scofield. 12mo, cloth, net 75c.

"Anything that comes from the pen of this writer and Bible teacher may be accepted as thoroughly sound and intelligent in its presentation of truth. This is a study of the historical and prophetic aspects of the kingdom of God in their relations to the present age and that which is shortly to come."—*Christian Worker's Magazine.*

REV. D. M. CANRIGHT

The Complete Testimony

The Testimony of the Early Fathers, Proving the Universal Observance of Sunday in the First Centuries. 12mo, paper, net 20c.

The author of "Seventh Day Adventism" gives in concise, connected form the testimonies of all the early Christian Fathers from the Apostles down to A. D. 400. Invaluable to pastor and people—there is no other booklet like it.

C. F. WIMBERLY, B.A.

Behold the Morning!

The Imminent and Premillennial Coming of Jesus Christ. 12mo, cloth, net $1.15.

R A. Torrey says: "I am sure the book will interest a great many in the subject, who have not been interested in the ordinary discussions of the subject. The book is one of the three books that I would recommend to any one who wishes to take up a study of the subject."

HENRY T. SELL, D.D.

Bible Studies in Vital Questions

12mo, cloth, net 60c; paper, net 35c.

The new volume of Sell's Bible Studies is prepared for adult Bible and pastors' classes and for use in schools, colleges and private study. It deals, in a plain, concise and constructive way, with the vital questions of the Christian faith about the Bible, God, Man and the Church. I. Vital Questions About the Bible. II. Vital Questions About God. III. Vital Questions About Man. IV. Vital Questions About the Church.

EDWARD LEIGH PELL

Author of "Pell's Notes on the Sunday School Lesson"

Our Troublesome Religious Questions

12mo, cloth, net $1.35.

A frank, earnest inquiry into, and discussion of, the problems of religious creed and conduct which vex and perplex believer and unbeliever alike. The author displays a marked ability to take up these questions and examine them with sagacity, impartiality and an optimistic, triumphant faith.